The Open University

A207
From Enlightenment to Romanticism, *c.*1780–1830

Block 5 Davy and Soane: New Approaches to Science and Architecture

This publication forms part of an Open University course A207 *From Enlightenment to Romanticism, c.1780–1830*. Details of this and other Open University courses can be obtained from the Course Information and Advice Centre, PO Box 724, The Open University, Milton Keynes MK7 6ZS, United Kingdom: tel. +44 (0)1908 653231, e-mail general-enquiries@open.ac.uk

Alternatively, you may visit the Open University website at http://www.open.ac.uk where you can learn more about the wide range of courses and packs offered at all levels by The Open University.

To purchase a selection of Open University course materials visit the webshop at www.ouw.co.uk, or contact Open University Worldwide, Michael Young Building, Walton Hall, Milton Keynes MK7 6AA, United Kingdom for a brochure. tel. +44 (0)1908 858785; fax +44 (0)1908 858787; e-mail ouwenq@open.ac.uk

The Open University
Walton Hall, Milton Keynes
MK7 6AA

First published 2004

Edited, designed and typeset by The Open University.

Printed and bound in the United Kingdom by the Alden Press, Oxford.

ISBN 0 7492 8599 0

1.1

Contents

Introduction to Block 5

Prepared for the course team by Gerrylynn K. Roberts

You have reached the beginning of the final third of your work on the transition 'From Enlightenment to Romanticism'. It will by now be clear that that transition was by no means a smooth, linear one and that the life and work of many individuals exemplified, without contradiction, characteristics of both. The individuals you will study in Block 5 are no exception. *Davy and Soane: New Approaches to Science and Architecture* focuses on two individuals from relatively modest backgrounds who became eminent in their respective fields of science and architecture by means of talent, systematic self-education, hard work and, it has to be said, some lucky breaks. As a consequence, both gained entry to metropolitan high society and received the highest honours available to them. However, despite their very considerable achievements and the fact that they were both popular educators, neither of them founded an enduring school of thought nor altered significantly at the time the development of their respective fields. Both lives spanned the period of the course. One of them is characterized explicitly in the units as an 'Enlightenment Romantic', and the description is apt for both. In Block 5 you will study not only individuals, but also the institutions with which they were associated or which they created, and through which they expressed themselves in a period when the way that both science and architecture were pursued was changing rapidly.

In Units 20–21 Gerrylynn Roberts considers the life and scientific activities of Sir Humphry Davy, analyzing them in relation to the role of science in society during his lifetime. Davy's career took place at the Royal Institution, which was founded in 1799 with the Enlightenment aim of applying science for bettering the lot of humankind through education and by means of a programme of scientific research on topics of practical relevance. Davy understood his audience and exploited its interests to pursue what we would now call more fundamental research as well. Davy was a chemist, and you will therefore be studying the development of some early nineteenth-century chemical ideas. Nowadays, we think of science as highly specialized knowledge, which can only properly be understood and pursued by experts who have had years of training. In the early nineteenth century, however, a broad understanding of scientific principles was characteristic of an educated person. It was during this period that science started to become more formally divided into separate subject areas. Chemistry was an exciting new scientific discipline in Davy's time, and he was heavily involved in working through the implications of recent chemical developments in France. As an independent science, not only was it of potentially wide-ranging, practical relevance, but it was intellectually exciting in its promise to explain the fundamental nature of matter. Consequently, it was the subject of many popular treatments at the time, one of which, by Jane Marcet, you will study.

You needn't worry about the scientific details, but should focus instead on the broad principles under discussion and the ways that these relate to the themes of the course. Davy was very much an Enlightenment figure in believing that scientific knowledge was progressive, should be studied by means of experiment, and should be used to improve the fortunes of humankind. He also felt that the study of nature would lead to a better understanding of God. At the same time, Davy displayed characteristics that could be called Romantic – an individually sensitive response to the poetic as well as the sublime in nature, a strong sense of self coupled with belief in individual genius displayed by an autobiographical approach to recording his work. Furthermore, he believed in an underlying dynamic force or power in nature, which might eventually offer a unifying explanation of all natural phenomena.

Should you feel it necessary to check your understanding of the science discussed in modern terms, you might like to consult *Oxford Reference Online*, which you can access via the OU Library resources on your eDesktop, though any standard printed encyclopaedia should be helpful. Modern chemists no longer understand certain phenomena in the way that Davy did, but we must not therefore interpret Davy as having been 'wrong' in the modern sense, or even as having been 'right', in some of his work. The important thing is to understand Davy's work in the context of his own time. This context included both the Industrial Revolution and the French Revolution. The former reinforced the Enlightenment desire to apply chemistry, while the latter engendered a fear that new chemical ideas coming from France might be radical and subversive. Strictly, it is even anachronistic to describe Davy as a 'scientist', since the term was not coined until shortly after his death, though the new word was meant to encapsulate the characteristics of the very type of career that he had created and pursued.

In Units 22–23 Tim Benton looks at the life and architectural activities of Sir John Soane. Already an adult by the time of Davy's birth, Soane too made his own way within an emerging career possibility of the time, that of professional architect. Soane's was also a career that combined theory and practice. His architecture moved from a typically Enlightenment learned classicism to a highly individual manner of exploring new possibilities of structure and lighting. Thus he held an Enlightenment belief in the acquisition of knowledge and the perfectibility of people and things by the application of reason and all but venerated classical architectural forms. At the same time, however, his reputation rests on what he called the search for 'character' in a building, in other words the individuality and originality with which an architect applied and interpreted those forms – a Romantic quality. Typically for an architect of his day, Soane learned through apprenticeship and by studying past examples. He travelled extensively in Italy and was especially influenced by ancient Roman archaeological sites, as well as by the friends and patrons he gained there and the stock of detailed drawings which he made. Subsequently gaining important commissions in Britain, Soane set about establishing his own collection of paintings and antiquities, deliberately positioning himself as a member of the artistic and intellectual elite of London. He attained in 1802 full membership of the Royal Academy, at which he would subsequently become Professor of Architecture in 1806. His professorship was marred by controversy, both intellectual and personal, for Soane always found it difficult to resolve the tensions between respect for the best models of antiquity and the need to innovate in his own architectural work.

Among the best exemplars of Soane's achievements, as well as of the tensions and contradictions in his work and thinking, are Soane's own London home in Lincoln's Inn Fields and the museum he developed there over a period of years. Located conveniently near to the Royal Academy, it gradually expanded from the house he purchased initially to include a number of adjacent properties. Its collection of antiquities, both casts and fragments, architectural drawings and paintings enabled Soane to claim that his collection rivalled that of the British Museum. More than just a place of display or statement of Soane's view of himself, the museum was also a place of work providing inspiration and models for his students. It also became a repository of Soane's own drawings. The museum is an important text for Units 22–23. It is an expression of an Enlightenment desire to increase and document with evidence human knowledge, but also a highly charged and poetic artistic statement.

Block 5 is unusual in the course in that each of its pairs of units has an integral CD-ROM, and there is an associated Activities Booklet which supports your work on the respective CD-ROMs in different ways. We would encourage you to have a go, if possible, but have provided alternative learning experiences for those of you who may not be able to use the CD-ROMs for whatever reasons. The two CD-ROMs are quite different in approach. That devoted to 'Science as Public Culture' is the more didactic in style, aiming to help you understand early nineteenth-century chemistry and the settings in which it took place by using animations of a contemporary popularizing text together with video reconstructions of some important experiments and locations. The CD-ROM devoted to 'Sir John Soane's Museum' enables you to explore this exciting building and monument to Soane's life and work quite freely. You can move around panoramic images of rooms, zoom for detailed views of objects and look up items in the database. A range of exercises in the Activities Booklet will guide you through the resources in a more structured way. The two CD-ROMs do have, where possible, certain design features in common to facilitate your use of them, and the points at which you are expected to use them, or pursue an alternative, are clearly indicated in your units.

Units 20–21
Science as public culture

Prepared for the course team by Gerrylynn K. Roberts

Contents

Study components

Weeks of study	*Supplementary material*	*Audio-visual*	*Anthologies and set books*	*CD-ROM*
2	Activities Booklet Illustrations Book	–	Anthology II	*Science as Public Culture*

Some of the exercises in these units direct you to activities on the *Science as Public Culture* CD-ROM. The Activities Booklet contains instructions on how to install the CD-ROM, and the CD-ROM itself includes an explanation of the structure of the material and how you should study it in 'How to use this CD-ROM', which you should work through first before attempting any activities. For those of you who are unable to use the CD-ROM, the Activities Booklet also contains an Alternative Learning Experience (ALE) for every computer-based activity.

Aims

1 To examine how scientific – in this case chemical – knowledge is embedded in its particular temporal and cultural contexts.

2 To explore through the life of a prominent chemist, Humphry Davy:

- the emergence during this period of the scientific career, that is to say, the 'scientist';
- a set of important chemical discoveries;
- the role of the scientist as an actor in the wider culture.

3 To investigate, by studying the Royal Institution, the development of scientific institutions.

Objectives

By the end of your work on Units 20–21 you should be able:

- to give examples of what it means to talk about 'Enlightenment chemistry' and 'Romantic chemistry' in Britain;
- to explain the influence of the French Revolution on British science;
- to explain why chemistry achieved popularity in Britain during this period;
- to explain what is meant by the term 'public science' as used by historians.

1 Introduction: science and its publics

Chemistry was a hot topic of conversation in polite – that is, middle- and upper-class – society in early nineteenth-century Britain. For the science, it was a time of ferment stimulated by empirical developments in Britain, theoretical developments in France, and the emergence of a new scientific instrument in Italy. At the same time, from the Enlightenment onwards, chemistry, of all sciences, seemed to offer particular scope for applications in Britain's industrializing economy, which was also dealing with the challenges of war with France. Chemical lecture series at new metropolitan institutions for educating the general public about science were attended to the point of overcrowding, while the publication of widely read chemical dictionaries, handbooks, catechisms, manuals and primers aimed at a popular audience amounted to a small industry.

Why and how this came to be the case is the subject of these units. We focus on the scientific career of Humphry Davy (1778–1829), whose life's span was nearly that of the period of A207. On one level, his biography is, if not quite a story of 'rags to riches', one of an individual whose enthusiasm for nature and talent as an experimenter took him from relatively modest Cornish beginnings to a position of wealth and prestige in London society. We will look especially at Davy's work at the Royal Institution of Great Britain (RI), which was founded in London in 1799 – near the midpoint of the course. The RI still thrives at its original Mayfair address. Indeed, you may be familiar with one of its high-profile public activities: the televising of its Christmas lectures for children by a different prominent scientist each year.

The first of your two Anthology texts, 'A discourse introductory to a course of lectures on chemistry', is the complete text of a lecture at the Royal Institution that was published shortly after Davy delivered it in 1802, just before his promotion to Professor of Chemistry. It is Davy's scientific manifesto, but also a manifesto for the fledgling RI. The second text is a set of extracts from Mrs Jane Marcet's[1] *Conversations on Chemistry*, which was first published in 1806 with the purpose of giving members of polite society, especially ladies, the necessary basic chemical background for better understanding Davy's lecture courses at the RI. It was a 'bestseller' reaching a tenth edition, from which your extracts are taken, in 1825. Davy approved of Mrs Marcet's efforts and apparently helped with this edition. There is also a sense in which the Royal Institution itself, both as a physical setting for and an exemplification of early nineteenth-century science, is a text for these units. You will explore this building, and look at others, on the 'Sites of science' section of the CD-ROM or in the Activities Booklet. Finally, in 'A dictionary of chemistry' on the CD-ROM or in the Activities Booklet, you will investigate another type of text, Davy's experiments. The CD-ROM

[1] Marcet is pronounced Mar-say.

demonstrates the experiments both as they were performed in the grand public lecture theatre of the Royal Institution and as they were described by Mrs Marcet to be studied in the domestic space of the Regency drawing room. In effect, this provides an early twenty-first-century domestic equivalent of what Mrs Marcet offered to her early nineteenth-century readers.

We will be looking at how science was presented to and understood by its audiences during the period of the course. We will be concerned with the ways in which science – produced in the private space of the laboratory by experiments – was made public knowledge and thereby earned its authority. The book from which the title of these units is borrowed, *Science as Public Culture: Chemistry and Enlightenment in Britain, 1760–1820* (Golinski, 1992), argues that the kinds of audiences available for experimental science in turn affected the way it could be communicated and therefore affected what became public knowledge. In Davy at the RI, you will be studying a natural philosopher – that is, as you may recall from Units 12–13, someone who studied science – who self-consciously exploited the audiences for chemistry in the early nineteenth century to further both his subject and his career.

2 Science as public culture in the eighteenth century

Itinerant lecturers and natural philosophy

Itinerant lecturers provided an important channel for communicating science and thus winning an audience for it in eighteenth-century English society. They interpreted the highly mathematical and abstruse work of Isaac Newton to the populace through expository texts, lectures and experimental demonstrations. In order to win acceptance for natural philosophy – which was the contemporary term for the physical sciences – they associated the subject with a range of technological activities to which their provincial audiences could relate (Stewart, 1992). A very famous representation of an itinerant lecturer, though in a domestic setting rather than a public lecture room, is Joseph Wright's *An Experiment on a Bird in the Air Pump* of 1768 (see Plate 20.1 in the Illustrations Book).

EXERCISE Study Plate 20.1 and consider the following questions:

1 In what different ways is science being communicated to the viewer of the painting?

2 In what ways is this painting a representation of the Enlightenment?

DISCUSSION

1 Perhaps most obviously, the lecturer depicted is demonstrating a particular experiment to a particular audience, so on one level the viewer is being informed about both the elements of that demonstration and how science was communicated to that audience. On another level, however, Wright is interpreting the experience of that scientific demonstration for his own audience by means of such elements as composition, the choice of scientific detail, the lighting, the response of the audience depicted, etc.

2 The painting exemplifies the Enlightenment principle discussed in Units 4 and 5 that the criterion of knowledge should be directly experienced evidence, in this case a predictable demonstration of experimental evidence. At the same time, Wright portrays his audience as being literally enlightened, or at any rate illuminated, by the central light source at the base of the experimental apparatus.

There is another dimension to this last answer: though what Wright shows here is an experimental demonstration of existing knowledge rather than the production by experiment of new knowledge, he was himself experimenting in this painting with the effects of light, another subject of Newtonian natural philosophy. Of course, he was also operating within precedents of artistic practice on the use of light, as well as other artistic traditions.

From a middle-class Derby family, Joseph Wright trained as a portrait painter in London and set up a studio in his home-town in the 1750s. In common with many prosperous manufacturing and trading towns in the Midlands and North of England, Derby had a rich scientific culture (Elliott, 2000). As elsewhere, manufacturers, merchants and professionals sought, through education in science, especially Newtonian natural philosophy, to achieve independent public status separate from that of the aristocracy. At the same time, what was understood to be the inherent utility of science justified their enthusiasm for innovation and affirmed the rightness of their actions in fostering industrialization. Attending the presentations of itinerant lecturers on natural philosophy and watching (and perhaps repeating) their experiments were the public means through which provincials could express these cultural ambitions. In turn, their prosperity funded such activities as they became consumers of science, purchasing books, instruments and apparatus and subscribing to lecture series (Porter, 1980). And this form of public participation in natural philosophy gave science its legitimacy (Stewart, 1992).

Through his acquaintance with a local clockmaker and geologist who would become a Fellow of the Royal Society, Wright became associated beyond Derby with the loose circle of Midlands medical men, inventors, entrepreneurs and others interested in natural philosophy later known collectively as the Lunar Society of Birmingham. (The group was so-called because it met monthly on the Monday closest to the full moon for ease of homeward travel.) This Enlightenment group included pottery manufacturer Josiah Wedgwood; silversmith, assayer and coinmaker Matthew Boulton, who would become a pioneering steam-engine manufacturer with another member, James Watt; doctor, poet and natural philosopher Erasmus Darwin; and literary figures such as Thomas Lovell Edgeworth, a writer on education and transport. They were humanitarians, some of whom would support the cause of abolition (see Figure 20.1). They were firm believers that advancement for humanity could be achieved through scientific knowledge and the harnessing of nature. The atmosphere of their gatherings is well described in a letter written by Darwin to Boulton apologizing for having to miss one: 'What inventions, what wit, what rhetoric, metaphysical, mechanical, & pyrotechnical, will be on the wing, bandyed like a shuttlecock from one to another of your troop of philosophers!' (quoted in Uglow, 2002, p.265). Philosophers in this case means 'natural philosophers'. The members discussed the latest developments in natural philosophy, performed experiments and considered technological projects. Wright was not a member of the Lunar Society himself, but he received portrait commissions from some of them. His scenes of scientific studies represented their interests and indeed represented people like them.

Figure 20.1 Anonymous, Am I Not a Man and a Brother?, *1787, ceramic medallion, Wedgwood Museum Trust Limited, Barlaston. Photo: by courtesy of the Wedgwood Museum Trust Limited, Barlaston, Staffordshire.*

Commissioned by the newly formed Society for Effecting the Abolition of the Slave Trade, which Wedgwood joined, and executed by his firm, these pottery cameos were shipped by him in their thousands to Benjamin Franklin in Philadelphia for free distribution in support of the abolitionist cause. Apparently, they became a 'must have accessory' and were very effective publicity. The image in fact became the symbol of the anti-slavery movement, although the Society was committed only to the abolition of the trade. However, the image conveyed a mixed message, for while the kneeling figure was meant to be at prayer, it could also be read as portraying the slave as a supplicant to white society (WGBH Interactive, 1998, online).

EXERCISE Look now at the venues and activities of the Lunar Society on the 'Sites of science' section of the CD-ROM or in the Activities Booklet (ALE 1). Consult your Activities Booklet for instructions on how to install the CD-ROM, and work through 'How to use this CD-ROM' before attempting this exercise.

The **air pump** shown in Plate 20.1 (see Illustrations Book) was a key device in the armoury of the itinerant lecturer. Itself an object for investigation in the seventeenth century, it had by the mid-eighteenth century become a standard instrument for probing nature and demonstrating the mechanical properties of air (pneumatics). The acceptance of such an instrument as standard made it possible for the experiments of natural philosophers to be repeated, shared and checked in public. It thus became possible to make science public knowledge by means of experimental demonstration (Shapin and Schaffer, 1985). Wright is thought to have attended the Derby lectures of 1762 by a famous itinerant lecturer, James Ferguson, who is known to have had an air pump.

In the domestic version of the experiment painted by Wright, we see a family's ornamental caged bird, a cockatoo, which has been removed from its cage and placed in a glass vessel from which the air has then been extracted by means of the air pump. We come to the scene when the bird is already near death at the bottom of the vessel. Unless the lecturer admits air by means of the stopcock in his left hand, the bird will die. This is a rather extreme form of the experiment, chosen by Wright for dramatic effect. Where live birds were used, they were usually common garden birds, not family pets, nor such exotic species as the cockatoo, which had only recently begun to be imported from the East Indies (Schupbach, 1987, p.347). Indeed, Ferguson thought it inappropriate to use live creatures at all in a demonstration to a polite audience:

> If a fowl, a cat, rat, mouse or bird be put under the receiver, and the air be exhausted, the animal is at first oppressed as with a great weight, then grows convulsed and at last expires in all the agonies of a most bitter and cruel death. But as this experiment is too shocking to every spectator who has the least degree of humanity, we substitute a machine called the lungs-glass in place of the animal; which, by a bladder within it, shews how the lungs of the animals are contracted into a small compass when the air is taken out of them [see Figure 20.2].
>
> (James Ferguson, 1760, quoted in Fraser, 1990, p.19)

Figure 20.2a Glass globe containing an inflated bladder, late eighteenth century, King George III Collection, Science Museum, London. Photo: Science and Society Picture Library, London.

Figure 20.2b Glass globe containing a deflated bladder, late eighteenth century, King George III Collection, Science Museum, London. Photo: Science and Society Picture Library, London.

The example shown here is from the collection of apparatus supplied to King George III for use in scientific demonstrations to the royal family. This consists of a bladder attached to a small pipe fixed inside a glass globe. Air can enter or leave the bladder via the pipe and a nozzle on top of the globe. Figure 20.2a shows a globe with the bladder inflated. When this is placed under the glass receiver on top of the air pump platform from which the air is then removed, the bladder is also emptied of air and collapses, as in Figure 20.2b. When air is allowed back in, the bladder expands. In fact, 'lungs-glass' (as referred to in the quote from Ferguson) was a misnomer because the apparatus does not demonstrate how lungs work (Morton and Wess, 1993, pp.281, 449–50).

EXERCISE Look again at Plate 20.1. Describe the reactions of the various members of the lecturer's audience to this dramatic version of the experiment. Compare their responses by gender.

DISCUSSION The experiment as Wright shows it certainly upsets the young girls as they contemplate the possible death of their pet. Their father is distracted from the experiment by comforting them, while urging them to look at it. The older gentleman on the right is not looking at the experiment, but seems to be lost in his own sombre thoughts, perhaps contemplating its implications. The young boy on the left displays a fascinated curiosity, while the young man next to him is timing the event in a detached, matter-of-fact manner. The young woman of the courting couple ignores the experiment altogether. In fact, none of the females in the picture is really engaging with the experiment.

In contemporary constructions of sentiment and sensibility, women were identified as the more feeling sex, perhaps more compassionate than rational. Solkin (1992, p.94) suggests that there is a figure 'missing' from the painting – the mother of the young girls, the lady of the house. Participating in the acquiring of knowledge was not her role; that was to create an ordered household for her family. Wright's choice of the more dramatic form invoked the contemporary notion of the sublime, a response of fear and awe in the face of nature, which you encountered in Units 16 and 17. Furthermore, using a live bird emphasizes that it is nature that is at issue here rather than mechanical devices. A further contrast of artifice with nature is the full moon, slightly obscured by cloud, which can be seen through the window. This is sometimes construed as an explicit reference to the Lunar Society. Though the group had not yet attracted that name by 1768, it had established the practice of travelling on moonlit nights.

But the painting is more than a representation of science in a particular setting. Wright painted it for exhibition and sale at the Society of Artists in London, where it would be seen by thousands and might also attract the attention of the reproductive print trade (Solkin, 1992, p.89). It was thus a commercial painting with strong moral and religious dimensions in its contemporary setting. In the first place, such scientific demonstrations themselves had a moral purpose. In the painting Wright includes a commentary on this middle-class audience for science. Three generations are depicted in the scene, indicating the span of life, along with various reminders of mortality and its unpredictability. The older gentleman's sombre mood fits this reading. Notice the rod leading directly from the lecturer's pointing finger to the vessel with the skull in the centre of the table. In fact, a skull is not likely to have been an accompaniment to a lecture on pneumatics. The skull, silhouetted here by candlelight from behind, and the candle, a reflection of which can be seen on the side of the vessel, are drawn from traditional iconography, the first representing death and the second representing the passage of time. Together they point to the vanity of human pleasures – in this case, coming together for the sake of improvement by learning about natural philosophy (Schupbach, 1987, p.346). Furthermore, the imperial source of the bird is perhaps a reference to the source of the wealth of some middle-class English provincials.

The scientific element at the heart of this painting is the fate of the bird, which also provides the significant moment in the work, when the fate of individuals hangs in the balance. Will the natural philosopher allow the bird to live or let it die (Egerton, 1990, pp.58–61)? Alarmingly, through science he has the power to do either. What are the limits to the power of natural philosophy? Fraser (1990, p.20) suggests that the central grouping of the father figure pointing to the bird, taken together with the gesture of the lecturer towards the viewer, represents the Trinity of Father, Holy Spirit and Christ (reaching out). This reading also helps to explain the choice for the experiment of a (pure) white bird which has come from afar over a common garden bird – a white dove often represented the Holy Spirit.

EXERCISE How does Fraser's analysis of the association of religious imagery with scientific experiment in Wright's painting fit with the discussion of natural religion in Unit 4 (pp.173–9) and in Units 12–13 (pp.121–4)?

DISCUSSION The association of religious imagery with scientific experiment may be seen as an expression of the contemporary view that the study of nature's laws revealed the operations of God and therefore brought humanity closer to knowledge of God.

Joseph Priestley and pneumatic chemistry as public knowledge

It was through the work of Joseph Priestley (1733–1804), metaphysician, radical, political writer, Unitarian minister, theologian and natural philosopher, that chemistry entered the realm of public knowledge in the eighteenth century. In addition to working as a clergyman, Priestley had spells working as a teacher of various subjects in Dissenting academies and as a librarian to a wealthy Wiltshire landowner in whose house he had a private laboratory. It was here that, during the 1770s, he did some of his most famous chemical experiments. Priestley deliberately distanced himself from the metropolitan **Royal Society** – though elected a member – and its associations with the state and the London scientific establishment. Priestley was in Birmingham during the 1780s, enjoying membership in and patronage from the Lunar Society. Their support and interest provided him not only with some funds but also with a stimulating audience for his work. He recognized this himself, acknowledging to Josiah Wedgwood: 'For the pleasure of communicating our discoveries is one great means of engaging us to enter upon and pursue such laborious investigations' (quoted in Golinski, 1992, p.67). In other words, he was conscious that an 'audience' affected his work.

Though 'chemist' is not a disciplinary label that fitted Priestley at the time, his experimental work on the chemical properties of a variety of airs (gases) – that is, 'pneumatic' chemistry – has led to his being seen historically as a chemist. Most famous is his discovery in 1774 of what we now call oxygen. The tool he developed for studying airs, the pneumatic trough, by means of which the gases could be handled, opened them up to chemical investigation. The new tool also opened up Priestley's own experiments for repetition and display on the itinerant lecture circuit, whose venues were expanded from the early 1780s by the establishment of new literary and philosophical societies in many industrial towns. (Derby's was founded in 1784.) The demonstration of the chemical properties of air with the pneumatic trough complemented the study of the mechanical properties of air with the air pump. Priestley conducted his chemical researches within the conceptual framework of the phlogiston theory, which was first articulated in the seventeenth century. This theory explained many observed chemical phenomena, especially those of combustion (or burning), in terms of a hypothetical substance, 'phlogiston'. This was thought to have negative weight and was apparently given off when a substance was burned in air, thus accounting for its observed weight gain.

EXERCISE To understand the physical setting of Priestley's work go to 'Sites of science' on the CD-ROM or the Activities Booklet (ALE 2). You should also examine how the pneumatic trough works in 'A dictionary of chemistry' on the CD-ROM or in the Activities Booklet (ALE 3).

Priestley himself made his science public through his work as a writer, publishing carefully prepared texts narrating the sequence of experimental processes by which he established what he saw as the incontrovertible facts of science, so that they could be reproduced by his readers for themselves with minimal equipment. His was a thoroughly Enlightenment agenda. He eschewed scientific theory but had a radical agenda for spreading knowledge of experimental science throughout society:

> The rapid progress of knowledge ... will, I doubt not, be the means, under God, of extirpating all error and prejudice, and of putting an end to all undue and usurped authority in the business of religion as well as of science; and all the efforts of the interested friends of corrupt establishments of all kinds, will be ineffectual for their support in this enlightened age ... And the English hierarchy (if there be anything unsound in its constitution) has equal reason to tremble even at an air pump, or an electrical machine.
>
> (Quoted in Golinski, 1992, p.81)

Arguing thus for science as an instrument of political and religious change, it is not surprising that Priestley was a supporter of the French Revolution. In 1791 he replied publicly to Edmund Burke's *Reflections on the Revolution in Europe* of 1790, not only supporting the revolution but also advocating the rights of man and individual liberty while opposing the Established Church (Crosland, 1987, p.283) (see Figure 20.3). Priestley's Birmingham house and meeting place were consequently stormed by an angry mob on the second anniversary of the storming of the Bastille. He fled to the Dissenting community in London and emigrated to America in 1794.

Figure 20.3 Anonymous, Priestley as Doctor Phlogiston, *1791, Department of Prints and Drawings, British Museum, London. Photo: by courtesy of the Trustees of the British Museum, London.*

This is one of a number of caricatures of Priestley stimulated by Burke's hostile rhetoric (Golinski, 1992, pp.176–84). Among other barbs, Burke accused experimenters of being inhumane, implicating the air pump and pneumatic chemistry: 'The philosophers consider man in their experiments no more than they do mice in an air pump, or in a recipient of mephitic gas [which does not support respiration so the mouse would die]' (quoted in Golinski, 1992, p.178). Priestley is depicted brandishing political and religious tracts which give out nasty smoke. His pockets are stuffed with 'revolution toasts', 'Essays on matter and spirit' and a document labelled 'Gunpowder'. The last referred to Priestley's mentioning gunpowder metaphorically in a political context in a sermon of 1787, which earned him the sobriquet 'Gunpowder Joe' and aroused suspicion and further hostility (Crosland, 1987, pp.285–8).

3 Humphry Davy in the provinces

Cornish youth

It was into the very different provincial context of Penzance in rural Cornwall that Humphry Davy was born in 1778, the first of five children. The family was of respectable background, but Davy's father made a number of unfortunate financial decisions. When he died young, his widow opened a millinery shop to pay off the family debts. Young Humphry was clearly bright and personable, and he became the protégé of members of the family's local professional middle-class connections. For example, he attended the grammar school in Truro for a year, paid for by a local surgeon-apothecary. During these early years, Davy developed a great love of the outdoors stimulated by the rugged Cornish landscape. He became a keen angler, an excellent shot and an enthusiastic amateur geologist, all interests that would be lifelong. Engagement with his surroundings also gave Davy an appreciation of industry and technological innovation. At the end of the eighteenth century, bronze (an alloy of tin and copper) was still a widely used metallurgical product of considerable economic importance. Historians' tendency to concentrate on the innovative technologies of the Industrial Revolution in this period, such as iron making, sometimes obscures the continuing contemporary economic role of mature technologies, such as tin metallurgy. Replacement of an existing mature technology by a new one is seldom instantaneous. Cornwall was the principal tin-mining area in the country. Though a mature industry, tin mining was still technologically innovative. It was to the established Cornish tin mines, which faced flooding problems because of the need to go ever deeper to find more ore, that that icon of the Industrial Revolution, the steam engine, was first marketed for pumping. Cornish mines provided a key early market for Boulton and Watt's engines. There had long been a Cornwall–Midlands commercial axis, with Cornwall supplying the metallic raw materials for the workshops of Birmingham. At one level, the steam engine was the most up-to-date example of this technological and commercial nexus, with direct links between educated Cornish professionals and Lunar Society members.

EXERCISE Explore the physical setting of Davy's early scientific and technological framework on the 'Sites of science' section of the CD-ROM or in the Activities Booklet (ALE 4).

At the age of 17, Davy took up an apprenticeship with an apothecary-surgeon who was a prominent citizen of Penzance. The plan was that he would follow the apprenticeship with a medical degree at Edinburgh, like Mungo Park and for similar reasons. It was the financially sensible route for a young man of scientific inclinations but limited means. During this period, Davy set out a rugged reading programme for himself across a range of ten disciplines, several with subdivisions. The extent to which he followed this through is uncertain. However, he was known throughout his life as a speedy and voracious reader, and there is certainly direct evidence that at this time he read contemporary Scottish and English philosophers, including Hume and also David Hartley, the utilitarian exponent of **associationist psychology**. He also read older texts such as Francis Bacon's *New Organon* of 1620, the classic call for the extension of knowledge through the prosecution of scientific research by the collection and classification of observable phenomena and experimental results.

It was not until 1797 that Davy reached 'chemistry' on his list of topics under the subject heading 'My profession'. Chemistry was an essential subject for a medical student. He read two texts, provided through his Cornish contacts, which were very different in style and content, but were both key publications of the period, and in fact provided excellent grounding. The first was Antoine Lavoisier's *Traité élémentaire de chimie* of 1789, the seminal text of a movement historians sometimes refer to as the 'chemical revolution'. Davy read it in French, possibly to work on his language skills while he worked on his chemistry, though it had been translated into English in 1790 as *Elements of Chemistry in a New Systematic Order, Containing All the Modern Discoveries.* Lavoisier reorientated chemistry away from the central concept of phlogiston. Instead, he provided a new, quantitatively based conceptual framework involving the oxygen recently discovered by Priestley and Scheele. Oxygen was one of the new gases of pneumatic chemistry. Lavoisier argued on the basis of his experiments that it combined with a substance on burning, and it was this that accounted for the gain in weight. In this respect, Lavoisier was also a pneumatic chemist. To replace the unsystematic chemical nomenclature that had developed in an ad hoc way through practice over centuries, Lavoisier developed a new, simpler, rational nomenclature to express his reconceptualization. Another component of Lavoisier's reforms was his replacement of the four classical elements of earth, air, fire and water – from which, since ancient times, everything was thought to be composed – by a table of 33 chemical elements. These were each defined operationally in the laboratory as unique substances which could be broken down no further by chemical analysis. Problematically for many of his contemporaries, Lavoisier included heat and light, which were immaterial 'substances', in his list of elements.

EXERCISE Look now at the experimental basis of Lavoisier's oxygen theory of combustion on the 'Dictionary of chemistry' section of the CD-ROM or in the Activities Booklet (ALE 5).

Much of Davy's most important chemical work would be in response to Lavoisier. His starting point was the second chemical text which he read as part of his programme, William Nicholson's two-volume *Dictionary of Chemistry, Exhibiting the present state of Theory and Practice of that Science, its Application to Natural Philosophy, the Processes of Manufactures, Metallurgy, and Numerous other Arts dependant on the Properties and Habitudes of Bodies WITH a considerable number of Tables expressing the Elective Attractions, Specific Gravities, Comparative Heats, Component Parts, Combinations, and other Affections of the Objects of Chemical Research* (1795). Cumbersomely titled, this was a detailed reference work of more than 1,000 pages. It provided an up-to-date summary of current chemical knowledge, and articulated in a systematic way the confusion which attempts to work out the implications of Lavoisier's system had created among chemists over the previous six years.

Lavoisier had written for an audience of sophisticated chemical contemporaries. His work drew on elaborate experiments conducted with expensive apparatus that only similarly equipped chemists could repeat. By contrast, Nicholson's was a work of popularization; his audience was the beginner. Nicholson raised questions about, and presented alternative views of, the phenomena as interpreted by Lavoisier. Furthermore, he suggested experimental strategies for tackling the problems raised, and gave detailed instructions about how they might be performed using simple apparatus. 'Dictionary' is perhaps a misleading title for a twenty-first-century reader. It was more than a source of information, for it also outlined a programme of work to resolve the difficulties stimulated by Lavoisier.

From this time onwards, chemistry became Davy's principal focus. One of the first things that he followed up experimentally was Nicholson's suggestion that, contrary to Lavoisier, heat was not an element but might be a form of motion. Davy's researches were brought to the attention of Thomas Beddoes (1760–1808) by a mutual Cornish acquaintance in 1798. Beddoes was so impressed that the young chemist had tackled the great Lavoisier's ideas that he invited Davy to take up the post of Chemical Superintendent at his new Pneumatic Institution in Bristol, offering him the opportunity to use a well-equipped laboratory for the first time. As the Pneumatic Institution was dedicated to medical practice and there was also established medical teaching available in Bristol, it was intended that Davy keep up his medical studies as well. Davy immediately sought, and was granted, release from his medical apprenticeship in Penzance.

Davy in Bristol: a 'son of genius' at the Pneumatic Institution

Just short of 20, Davy made the transition from small-town life in Cornwall to Bristol, then England's second largest city, a major commercial and cultural centre. Raised in the West Midlands and acquainted with members of the Lunar circle, Beddoes had trained in medicine at Oxford, London and Edinburgh. Interested in chemistry, he set himself up extramurally in Oxford as a teacher of chemistry. However, Beddoes's radical political sympathies and public enthusiasm for the French Revolution dictated a prudent departure in 1793 from conservative Oxford to Bristol. There he started a medical practice and married a daughter of a member of the Lunar Society. Late eighteenth-century Bristol was a centre of campaigning radicalism and of Romanticism, a base for such figures as the poets Robert Southey and Samuel Taylor Coleridge, who were at that time political radicals though they later moved towards High Toryism. Beddoes joined in the pamphleteering, and the Beddoes household became a centre of radical Bristol society. Beddoes took care to make Davy welcome, introducing him to his radical circle and sharing in his further education through a programme of mutual reading.

For Beddoes, political radicalism and medical reform were closely related. The physician should be a scientific expert who treated his patients investigatively (Porter, 1992, ch.4). A characteristically Enlightenment figure, Beddoes thought experiment was the path to knowledge; research was the key and the future lay in the integration of laboratory experiments with clinical findings to create a progressive medicine. Furthermore, publication and the sharing of findings among practitioners were essential. They should not be kept private as commodities for commercial negotiation with patients. Beddoes saw the role of the patient, when ill, as accepting the expert's advice and, when healthy, as taking charge of their own lives to maintain health and prevent illness so that treatment would not be necessary in the first place. To achieve the latter and to avoid quackery, popular education was essential. Thus while one aim of his Pneumatic Institution was to pursue research, another was to provide education through lectures. Therapeutically, Beddoes concentrated on the development of pneumatic therapies in medicine – hence the name of his institution – that is, the administration of the new gases, especially oxygen, for healing. With the help of James Watt, who built the gas-manufacturing apparatus that would produce the therapeutic agents and whose daughter Beddoes had treated (unsuccessfully), the Pneumatic Institution opened in 1799 shortly after Davy's arrival. Wedgwood was the principal financial backer.

The basis of practice at the Pneumatic Institution was the theory of medicine of the Edinburgh physician John Brown, who arranged diseases along a linear scale from those that were the result of under-stimulus (asthenic) to those that were the result of over-stimulus (sthenic). Examples of the former were colic, rheumatism, cholera, epilepsy, typhus, gout and scurvy; the latter included diseases such as apoplexy, tuberculosis, chicken pox and catarrh. Stimulants such as alcohol were often prescribed for asthenic diseases, while the depressant, opium, was a characteristic prescription for sthenic diseases. Though he was not in full agreement with this scheme, the idea of a scale suggested quantitative possibilities for treatment, which provided a key link to chemistry for Beddoes. As Beddoes's chosen therapeutic agents, the new gases would be administered to counter the degree of over- or under-stimulation in relation to the particular disease that the patient presented. Lavoisier had shown, for example, that oxygen from the air entered the bloodstream during respiration and was carried to all parts of the body. It was a stimulant and would therefore be used for treating asthenic diseases (Fullmer, 2000, ch.7). Davy was responsible for experimenting with gases.

Nitrous oxide

Nitrous oxide was the first gas that Davy was set to investigate for its medical uses and therapeutic benefits. In fact, even before arriving in Bristol, he had challenged published claims that the gas was poisonous. He was his own experimental subject, inhaling various quantities of the gas of different degrees of purity and refining the design of the apparatus until he was sure that the procedure could be used reliably with other people. Davy adopted Priestley's style of reporting his experiments in diary-like detail so that the argument was built up as a form of autobiography. On Boxing Day 1799, he repeatedly inhaled huge quantities and noted the effects:

> By degrees, as the pleasurable sensation increased, I lost all connection with external things; trains of vivid visible images rapidly passed through my mind, and were connected with words in such a manner, as to produce perceptions perfectly novel. I existed in a world of newly connected and newly modified ideas ... My emotions were enthusiastic and sublime; ... I exclaimed ... '*Nothing exists but thoughts! – the universe is composed of impressions, ideas, pleasures and pains!*'
>
> (Davy, 1839b, pp.289–90; emphasis in the original)

The trials were extended to members of the Beddoes household and visiting friends. Members of the Lunar circle tried it not for medical purposes but to experience the heightened mental states noted by Davy. Immediately after his experience of the gas, the Romantic poet Robert Southey wrote to his younger brother:

> Oh, Tom! I have had some [nitrous oxide]; it made me laugh and tingle in every toe and finger tip. Davy has actually invented a

> new pleasure for which language has no name. Oh, Tom! I am going for more this evening; it makes one so strong and happy! And without any after-debility, but, instead of it, increased strength of mind and body. Oh, excellent air-bag! Tom, I am sure the air in heaven must be this wonder-working gas of delight!
>
> (Quoted in Fullmer, 2000, p.221)

Some months later, Southey sent a report of the same incident for inclusion as testimony in Davy's book of 1800, *Researches Chemical and Philosophical, chiefly concerning Nitrous Oxide ... and its Respiration.*

> In breathing the nitrous oxide, I could not distinguish between the first feelings it occasioned and an apprehension of which I was unable to divest myself. My first definite sensation was a dizziness, a fulness in the head, such as to induce a fear of falling. This was momentary. When I took the bag from my mouth, I immediately laughed. The laugh was involuntary but highly pleasureable, accompanied by a thrill all through me; and a tingling in my toes and fingers, a sensation perfectly new and delightful. I felt a fulness in my chest afterwards; and during the remainder of the day, imagined that my taste and hearing were more than commonly quick. Certain I am that I felt myself more than usually strong and cheerful.
>
> (Quoted in Davy, 1839b, pp.300–1)

EXERCISE

1 Compare the style and contents of the two accounts by Southey.

2 What do you think might have been the purpose of including such lay testimony as evidence in a work of natural philosophy?

DISCUSSION

1 The first is a private letter. It is an immediate, euphoric reaction, perhaps coloured by brotherly boasting, rather than a formal record of what occurred. The second recasts the experience as a report of what happened, suitably toned down for the purpose of presenting scientific results.

2 Including the evidence of influential public figures was probably intended to give prestige to the research programme and weight to the results in this aspect of Davy's research. Given the influence of the gas on the person inhaling it, we might of course wonder how accurate an observer Southey, or anyone who inhaled nitrous oxide, could have been of his own responses.

The section containing such testimonies in Davy's book is preceded by more than 400 pages of detailed reports of chemical experiments on the preparation, handling and properties of the various gaseous oxides of nitrogen. For Davy, the important scientific conclusion from this work was that, contrary to Lavoisier's views, the chemical behaviour of substances is not an inherent property of their elementary matter. Observing that most acids contain oxygen, Lavoisier had concluded that oxygen was the principle of acidity. Because he did comparative work on a whole series of compounds of nitrogen and oxygen which had wildly different properties and chemical behaviours, Davy concluded that the material properties of nitrogen and oxygen could not account for all the phenomena; there had to be an underlying 'power' at work.

The chemical experiments themselves were the private side of Davy's scientific work, which he brought before the public only in his text. By contrast, the inhalation experiments by prominent individuals were public displays. That many of those participating were members of Beddoes's and, by then, Davy's radical Bristol circle served to associate this kind of scientific work with radicalism. Furthermore, even in the more sober of Southey's two accounts, the impression created is one of heightened mental states, of emotion and entertainment rather than sober scientific investigation. It was the sensational side of the nitrous oxide work that impressed the contemporary public, and nitrous oxide 'parties' became quite fashionable.

That the more extreme effects of the inhalation of nitrous oxide were what attracted attention indicates the problem that Davy and Beddoes faced in making this science 'public'. The results of inhalation were impressionistic and difficult to record because the person actually experiencing the phenomena was in no state to note observations, and often would have only a hazy memory of what precisely had occurred. Beddoes tried to foster experimentation by other medical practitioners by arranging for the manufacture and sale of the apparatus so that they might try it. Indeed, Davy also ran some limited trials in a medical context, but they were inconclusive. Nitrous oxide, which came to be called 'laughing gas', remained known chiefly for its entertainment value until the 1840s, when its anaesthetic properties were recognized. In terms of John Brown's theory, Beddoes and Davy thought that nitrous oxide was an excitant, thus by definition having no properties of a soporific. This prevented their spotting its anaesthetic effects at the time. In terms of their own medical aims, Davy and Beddoes had reached a dead end; the nitrous oxide work resulted in Davy being uncomfortable with Brown's theory. Entertainment was a different form of public science.

Davy and Romanticism

Among others who inhaled nitrous oxide in order to experience its mind-altering effects was Southey's friend, the Romantic poet Samuel Taylor Coleridge. Coleridge had already moved away from Bristol by this time, but he met Davy through Bristol connections. Both poets thought highly of Davy, who by all accounts was an engaging companion and raconteur. They sought instruction from him on matters scientific, even though they regarded chemistry as a lesser intellectual activity. For Coleridge, chemistry was 'poetry realized in nature' (Levere, 1981). Importantly for Davy, they encouraged him in his writing of poetry, a mode of expression which he had begun to explore while in Cornwall and which would become a lifelong activity. Davy's *Sons of Genius*, from which a few stanzas are printed here, was written over 1795–6. Southey published it in 1799, though he said privately that he thought it 'tedious and feeble' (Fullmer, 2000, p.129). Historians have seen the poem as Davy's declaration of his life plan.

The Sons of Genius

...

While Superstition rules the vulgar soul,
  Forbids the energies of man to rise,
Rais'd far above her low, her mean control,
  Aspiring Genius seeks her native skies.

...

Inspired by her, the Sons of Genius rise
  Above all earthly thoughts, all vulgar care;
Wealth, power, and grandeur, they alike despise, –
  Enraptured by the good, the great, the fair.

...

Yet not alone delight the soft and fair,
  Alike the grander scenes of Nature move;
Yet not alone her beauties claim their care,
  The great, sublime, and terrible, they love.

...

To scan the laws of Nature, to explore
  The tranquil reign of mild philosophy;
Or on Newtonian wings to soar
  Through the bright regions of the starry sky.

...

From these pursuits the Sons of Genius scan
  The end of their creation; hence they know
The fair, sublime, immortal hopes of man,
  From whence alone undying pleasures glow.

By Science calm'd, over the peaceful soul,
  Bright with the eternal Wisdom's lucid ray,
Peace, meek of eye, extends her soft control,
  And drives the fury Passions far away.

...

Like the tumultuous billows of the sea
Succeed the generations of mankind;
Some in oblivious silence pass away,
And leave no vestige of their lives behind.

Others, like those proud waves which beat the shore,
A loud and momentary murmur raise;
But soon their transient glories are no more, –
No future ages echo with their praise.

Like yon proud rocks amidst the sea of time,
Superior, scorning all the billow's rage,
The living Sons of Genius stand sublime,
Th' immortal children of another age.

...

Their's is the glory of a lasting name,
The meed of Genius, and her living fire;
Their's is the laurel of eternal fame,
And their's the sweetness of the Muse's lyre.

(Quoted in Paris, 1831, vol.1, pp.16–20)

EXERCISE What is Davy's 'plan'? What influences on his outlook does Davy reveal?

DISCUSSION Davy declares his intention to take up the Baconian call and to make his permanent mark as a son of genius by studying sublime nature. The influence of Davy's Cornish environment is clear, as is the Romantic mode of his engagement with his subject. He is concerned with the development of the self, sees nature – to which an emotional response is appropriate – as sublime, and is concerned with immortality. At the same time, the first and sixth stanzas reveal the familiar Enlightenment notion of knowledge overcoming superstition and unruly passions, thus leading to progress.

Through Coleridge, Davy met Wordsworth. Davy saw the second edition of the *Lyrical Ballads* through the press in Bristol for them. Some historians have suggested that Davy's language altered as a result. On the other hand, Davy has been credited with influencing changes made to the introduction to a later edition (Sharrock, 1962).

Many aspects of Davy's work and life were influenced by Romanticism. Fundamental to his thinking were beliefs in the unity of nature and an active universe. For Davy, 'power' was a fundamental building block of nature; there was a single principle underlying the active universe.

However, Romanticism was also a set of behaviours. We have already seen how, based on a Romantic understanding of nature, Davy embraced the notion of 'genius' as a spur to creativity. As he himself outlined, his life was to be a quest for the glory of recognition that was due to 'sons of genius' (Lawrence, 1990). His autobiographical narrative style, displayed in the book on nitrous oxide, was consistent with the Romantic view of autobiography as the wellspring of creativity (Fullmer, 2000, p.228). The search for self-understanding was an important Romantic tenet.

The Voltaic pile

Writing in 1810, Davy would say of the Voltaic pile that its invention in 1800 had been 'an alarm-bell to experimenters in every part of Europe' (Fullmer, 2000, p.297). He himself had certainly reacted instantly to its sounding. Static electricity had been known for centuries and was studied increasingly during the eighteenth century when devices were developed to collect a charge, which could then be deployed to produce an effect. However, in March 1800 the development by Alessandro Volta of a device to produce current electricity, soon to be known as the Voltaic pile, was announced to the Royal Society. William Nicholson and William Carlisle constructed one almost immediately in London, and noticed that if wires at either end of the pile were placed in water, bubbles of gas were produced at the end of each wire when a current was flowing through the device. When collected, the gases were shown to be hydrogen and oxygen. One hypothesis was that electricity had decomposed water; this would be investigated by many chemists over the following six years.

EXERCISE Study now the Voltaic pile and the Voltaic battery on the 'Dictionary of chemistry' section of the CD-ROM or in the Activities Booklet (ALE 6).

Excited by the new phenomenon of current electricity, Davy considered it in the final appendix to his book on nitrous oxide. He came to the conclusion very quickly that chemical reactions depended in some way on the action of what was called 'galvanic fluid'; that is, they were somehow electrical in nature. Immediately the nitrous oxide book was off to the publisher, Davy began to experiment with a battery consisting of up to 110 pairs of plates provided for him by Beddoes. His initial concern was to study the device itself in order to understand how it worked, to optimize it so that it would become a readily usable tool for addressing nature. He sought a new instrument to perform chemical analyses. His conclusion this time was symmetrical with his earlier one: chemical reactions produced electrical effects. The Voltaic battery produced electricity by chemical means. Moreover, he anticipated that the relationship was quantitative. Between finishing the nitrous oxide book and leaving the Pneumatic Institution, Davy produced some seven papers on the subject. He had found a new research field, the one with which he would make his mark in London, where he moved to become assistant lecturer in chemistry at the new Royal Institution of Great Britain in March 1801.

Science in France

We have already seen how, from an early stage, Davy's chemistry was a response to French chemistry. Lavoisier had lost his head at the end of the Terror for political rather than scientific reasons. However, the Enlightenment view of scientific activity as highly valued carried on in France during the revolutionary period and afterwards; it was treated as fundamental to the progress of the state. In perhaps the ultimate 'application' of the programme of the *philosophes*, eminent natural philosophers, including chemists, were called into political as well as practical service by successive regimes – which in British eyes served only to emphasize the radical threat posed by science. Science had a rhetorical as well as a practical role under Napoleon.

Having published his electrical discovery by correspondence with the Royal Society in England, Volta sought and received special permission to present it to the First Class of the National Institute of France. This replaced, under the Directorate, the former Royal Academy of Sciences, which had been closely associated with the Old Regime. Volta presented his work for three days in November 1801, and Napoleon attended all three meetings. There are a number of representations of this episode. Plate 20.2, painted by Alexandre-Evariste Fragonard (1780–1850), turns up frequently in history of science books under various titles. Its date and provenance are as uncertain as its title. A.-E. Fragonard's reputation has been rather overshadowed by that of his famous father, the Rococo painter Jean-Honoré Fragonard (1732–1806), but in his own lifetime Alexandre-Evariste was a prolific and respected artist in several media and regularly submitted entries to the Salon (Matthiesen Gallery, 2001, online). The younger Fragonard developed an official career as a painter and sculptor during the empire, when he received important Napoleonic commissions. It was from this period that he began to move away from the Neoclassicism of his teacher Jacques-Louis David, towards some of the more painterly techniques learned from his father, especially regarding the use of light. It is likely that this painting was done after 1830, when Fragonard's official career resumed during the reign of Louis Philippe, who championed a Napoleonic legend for his own political purposes (Gauja and Delom, 1966).

EXERCISE Remind yourself of the discussion of representations of Napoleon in Block 2, Unit 9, especially sections 2 and 3. Then study Plate 20.2 in the Illustrations Book and answer the following questions:

1 How is Napoleon presented, and why do you think he is presented in this way?

2 What does the painting suggest to you about science under Napoleon?

DISCUSSION 1 Napoleon is apparently examining a Voltaic pile while its inventor, Alessandro Volta, explains it. The studious Napoleon is wearing civil rather than military uniform and is seated among people who, from their dress, would seem to be of similar status, members of French polite society. Napoleon does not stand out among them, apart from the edge of the broad shaft of daylight that falls directly upon him in literal enlightenment, but defers to the standing Volta's scientific knowledge. Napoleon is cast here as an 'enlightened' man: in this case, being enlightened about science. He is not depicted as 'doing' science. Not forgetting the artist's official role, here we have the head of state associated with the most advanced scientific knowledge for purposes of propaganda.

2 The painting was made some years after the event, so the specific details shown probably indicate very little about science at the time. However, the subject matter and its treatment suggest that up-to-date science was, at least for purposes of propaganda, taken seriously by the French state and that Napoleon wanted to be portrayed as a patron of science.

Images such as this, which retrieved the reputation of Napoleon, were common during the Restoration. A painting of Napoleon as a patron of science at a meeting of the First Class of the Institute may be seen as a gesture to align his image not only with Enlightenment values of scientific knowledge, but also with a function appropriate to his role. The Institute's pre-revolutionary predecessor, the Royal Academy of Sciences, enjoyed kingly patronage from its foundation in 1666 to its demise. However, the details of the setting and attendance at the meeting have been described as fanciful (Gauja and Delom, 1966).

On the other hand, Napoleon had sought and achieved election to the First Class of the Institute in December 1797. As was the case for artillery officers generally in France in the late eighteenth century, he had had a sound mathematical and engineering education, and was genuinely interested in science and aware of its development. Eighteen months later, he put it thus:

> I have used the imposing phrase 'dignity of science'. It is the only one which conveys my thought exactly. I know of no better way for a man to spend his life than to work to know nature and all things of use accessible to reason in the material world.
>
> (Quoted in Crosland, 1967, p.17)

However, Napoleon had little claim to scientific achievement himself, and his election over more qualified and accomplished candidates is generally seen as a political gesture to honour a national hero favoured by the government of the day. He took part, though minimally, in the Institute's activities, and shortly after becoming First Consul he served a six-month term as president of the First Class. The meeting with Volta was perhaps the apogee of Napoleon's direct involvement with the Institute. It is difficult to determine from the Fragonard painting, but it may well be the uniform of a member of the First Class that Napoleon is wearing.

According to the minutes of the first of the three meetings at which Volta spoke, it was proposed that:

> the [First] Class [of the Institute] should demonstrate its desire to gather together the wisdom of all those who cultivate the sciences, ... as a mark of its special esteem for this professor and of its great eagerness to welcome the work of all foreign scientists. He [Citizen Bonaparte] also proposed that a commission should be given the task by the Class of carrying out on a large scale all experiments which might throw a new light on the important branch of physics, which Citizen Volta has just expounded to the Class.
>
> (Quoted in Crosland, 1967, p.20)

Not only did the First Consul see it as important to associate the best, most up-to-date scientific work with France, but he was also prepared to exercise patronage to achieve specific ends. More utilitarian projects, such as extracting sugar from beet to replace that from West Indian cane made unavailable by war, would also be sponsored. French science thus flourished in the Napoleonic era not only to enhance the cultural prestige of France and its emperor but also to encourage its economy.

4 Humphry Davy in the metropolis: the early years

The Royal Institution

The Royal Institution was founded in the same year as the Pneumatic Institution, 1799, at the London home of Sir Joseph Banks. It was funded by private subscription of 50 guineas per member as an:

> Institution for diffusing the knowledge, and facilitating the general introduction, of useful mechanical inventions and improvements; and for teaching, by courses of philosophical lectures and experiments, the application of science to the common purposes of life.
>
> (Quoted in James, 2000, p.3)

EXERCISE

1. To what extent were the activities of the proposed institution scientific?
2. Does this sound like an institution of the Enlightenment?

DISCUSSION

1. The proposed institution was to be concerned with the diffusion of technical knowledge and innovations, and with the application of science to everyday life.
2. The short answer is 'yes': the diffusion of useful knowledge and the application of science for purposes of improvement were key Enlightenment values.

Notice that, initially, the Royal Institution was not promoted as a centre for scientific research. Given the discussion of the purposes of science in Units 12–13, the involvement of Sir Joseph Banks in this Enlightenment institution is hardly surprising. The broad historical context of the establishment of the RI is what has been called the 'dual revolution' which in fact you have been studying – the French Revolution and the Industrial Revolution. Agriculture was an important hoped-for area of improvement by means of the application of science, which attracted subscribers to the new institution. The number of proprietors (principal subscribers) increased to 280 in the first year. The demands of feeding a nation prevented by war from importing food fuelled the Enlightenment trend towards agricultural improvement. The English landowning aristocracy, especially those of a reforming persuasion who were also members of the Board of Agriculture and the Society for Bettering the Condition of the Poor,[2] became key supporters of the new institution, from which they expected scientific input to agricultural practice. For not

[2] The Board of Agriculture, established in 1793, was formed by a group of improving landlords who wished to bring science directly to bear on agricultural practice. It aimed to encourage all landowners and farmers to experiment. The Society for Bettering the Condition of the Poor was established in 1796 by improving landlords with the aim of providing the rural poor with allotments (and a cow) along with instructions about how to manage them on scientific principles. This aim was in part philanthropic, although the impulse behind it was to avert rural unrest while making the rural poor independent and therefore not a cost to landowners.

only was the application of science expected to improve landowners' agricultural incomes, but also the increase in food supplies would, it was argued, prevent French-style unrest by improving the lives of the poor. Furthermore, the diffusion of scientific knowledge and provision of practical tips to help the poor were seen as a strategy for relieving rural distress and therefore another means of forestalling social disruption. Benjamin Thompson, Count Rumford (a German title), whose own researches on the properties of heat had famously resulted in the invention of a fuel-efficient stove, was especially associated with this aspect of the proposal to establish what became the Royal Institution (Berman, 1978, ch.1).

The new institution found premises in a gentleman's large dwelling house in Albemarle Street, Mayfair. Figure 20.4, which shows the building in the late 1830s, is the earliest known image of it. In this watercolour, made to show off the brand new neoclassical façade, the building looks very much as it does now, with rendered brick and an imposing façade of 14 three-quarter round Corinthian columns. Apparently, it was modelled on the ruined *Tempio di Antonino* in Rome (see Figure 20.5). Neoclassical façades characterized a number of new intellectual institutions in London in the 1820s. In the period we are concerned with, however, the Royal Institution building looked very much like the house which can be seen to its right – substantial but rather less grand – a 'home' for science rather than a great institution. In some respects the early RI was rather like a gentleman's club, a number of which were quite close by in Mayfair. It had private rooms for members, including a reading room; early plans included a members' dining room, where fare from the proposed experimental kitchens was meant to be consumed.

The first Professor of Chemistry was Thomas Garnett (1766–1802). He was known in Scotland for his lectures on the applications of chemistry to agriculture as well as to such manufacturing processes as bleaching, calico printing and dyeing, all important supporting technologies of the key textile-manufacturing sector of the Industrial Revolution (see Units 18–19). Garnett's lecture courses, both fashionable and serious, began in the partly refurbished building on 4 March 1800 and immediately drew crowds including 'persons of the first distinction and fashion as well as ... those who had individually contributed much to the promotion of science' (quoted in Fullmer, 2000, p.327). As a consequence, carriage traffic was so heavy on lecture days that a one-way system was introduced in Albemarle Street in order to cope (see Figure 20.6). Though popular, the lectures were not universally approved. Lady Holland commented later that month on nitrous oxide demonstrations at the Royal Institution:

Figure 20.4 Thomas H. Shepherd, The Royal Institution of Great Britain, Albemarle Street, *c.1838, watercolour, 17 x 24.3 cm, Royal Institution, London. Photo: Bridgeman Art Library.*

The viewpoint chosen makes Albemarle Street look rather wider and more open than it was (or indeed is – there is room for a car to park either side and a single lane of traffic).

> This Institution of Rumford's furnishes ridiculous stories. The other day they tried the effect of the gas, so poetically described by Beddoes; it exhilarates the spirits, distends the machine [i.e. the body]. The first subject was a corpulent, middle-aged gentleman, who, after inhaling a sufficient dose, was requested to describe to the company his sensations; 'Why, I only feel stupid.' This intelligence was received amidst a burst of applause, most probably not for the novelty of the information. Sir Coxe Hippisley was the next who submitted to the operation, but the *effect* upon him was so *animating* that the ladies tittered, held up their hands, and declared themselves satisfied.
>
> (Quoted in Fullmer, 1960, p.12; emphasis in original)

Figure 20.5 Attributed to Laura Piranesi, Tempio di Antonino in Rome, *c.1780, etching, 13.6 x 20.3 cm, Royal Institution, London. Photo: Bridgeman Art Library.*

The choice of a classical model for the Royal Institution's alterations emphasized the equivalence in status of scientific knowledge with other sorts of knowledge. Several cultural institutions in the capital had neoclassical façades. University College London (then called the University of London) and King's College London, both founded in the 1820s, did, as did the new British Museum building, which was built over a period of some 25 years from the 1820s onwards.

Less than a year after the lectures started, Rumford recruited Davy, on the strength of his published researches, as Garnett's lecture assistant. As we have seen, Davy was at a point of transition in his research; he was ready to make the move. As Davy understood it, Rumford had given an undertaking that he would soon become a professor. Rumford also promised Davy full support for pursuing his own research interests (Fullmer, 2000, p.330).

EXERCISE How does this promise fit with the founders' objectives for the Royal Institution?

DISCUSSION On the one hand, the pursuit of scientific research seems to be an addition to the founders' objectives, which were focused on the diffusion

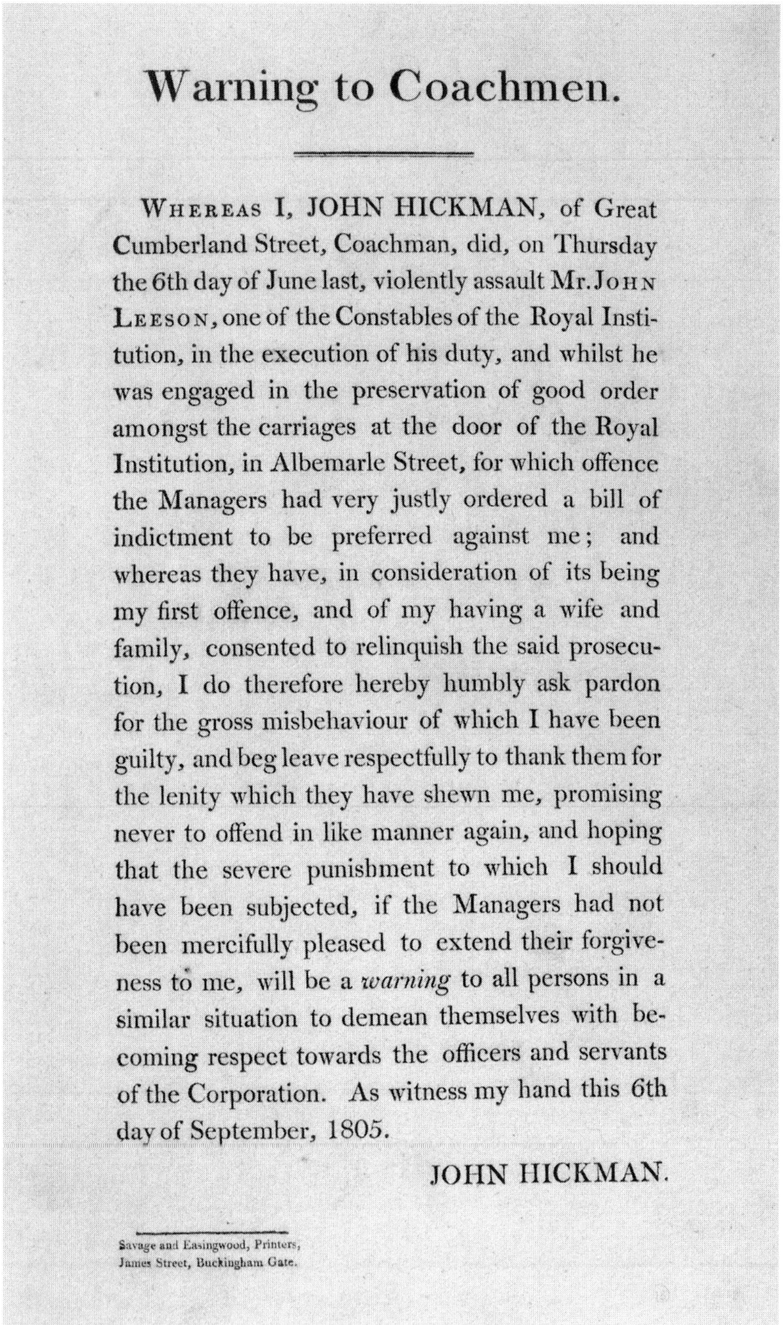

Warning to Coachmen.

Whereas I, JOHN HICKMAN, of Great Cumberland Street, Coachman, did, on Thursday the 6th day of June last, violently assault Mr. John Leeson, one of the Constables of the Royal Institution, in the execution of his duty, and whilst he was engaged in the preservation of good order amongst the carriages at the door of the Royal Institution, in Albemarle Street, for which offence the Managers had very justly ordered a bill of indictment to be preferred against me; and whereas they have, in consideration of its being my first offence, and of my having a wife and family, consented to relinquish the said prosecution, I do therefore hereby humbly ask pardon for the gross misbehaviour of which I have been guilty, and beg leave respectfully to thank them for the lenity which they have shewn me, promising never to offend in like manner again, and hoping that the severe punishment to which I should have been subjected, if the Managers had not been mercifully pleased to extend their forgiveness to me, will be a *warning* to all persons in a similar situation to demean themselves with becoming respect towards the officers and servants of the Corporation. As witness my hand this 6th day of September, 1805.

JOHN HICKMAN.

Savage and Easingwood, Printers,
James Street, Buckingham Gate.

Figure 20.6 Warning to Coachmen, *1805, 38 x 23.5 cm, Royal Institution, London. Photo: Bridgeman Art Library.*

This coachman's apology illustrates the traffic problem outside the Royal Institution. It is interesting that the RI employed constables at this time.

of useful knowledge and the applications of science. On the other hand, the production of scientific knowledge was an important strand of the Enlightenment, and such knowledge could be 'applied'.

In fact, Davy was recruited to a post that would involve high-profile public lecturing on the strength of his experimental researches and published work along with personal recommendations. He had done no lecturing in Bristol, but Fullmer argues that he would have been well prepared by the formal instruction in rhetoric and oratory which he had received in his Penzance days (2000, p.341). In his first season in the new lecture theatre of the Royal Institution, which could seat 900 people, he gave two series of lectures on electrical phenomena. Davy put the new electric battery through its paces in exciting demonstrations of sparks, flashes and colourful effects, while stressing that the new instrument would give experimenters the means to reveal nature's secrets. He was an instant hit. In May 1801 a review in the *Philosophical Magazine* commented approvingly:

> Mr. Davy, who appears to be very young, acquitted himself admirably well: from the sparkling intelligence of his eye, his animated manner and the *tout ensemble* [everything taken together], we have no doubt of his attaining a distinguished eminence.
>
> (*Philosophical Magazine*, vol.9, 1801, pp.281–2)

In June 1801 Davy gave a series of lectures on pneumatic chemistry. He commented on its success and on his comparative freedom at the RI in a letter to a friend:

> The voice of fame is still murmuring in my ears. My mind has been excited by the unexpected plaudits of the multitude – I dream of greatness & utility – ... My labours are finished for the season as to public experimenting and & public enunciation. My last lecture was on Saturday evening. Nearly 500 persons attended ... There was Respiration. Nitrous oxide: & unbounded applause. Amen. – To morrow a party of philosophers meet at the Institution, to inhale the joy inspiring gas. It has produced a great sensation ... I have been nobly treated by the Managers, God bless us I am about 1.000.000 times as much a being of my own volition as at Bristol.
>
> (Davy to Nicholas Jean [John] King, 22 June 1801, City of Bristol Archives, Bristol Record Office, ref. 32688/31)

In that same month Davy was promoted to lecturer, shortly before Garnett's resignation, and was requested by the managers to undertake the first of his applied tasks – a series of investigations followed by a series of lectures on the chemical principles of the art of tanning. This in fact was a request from the Board of Agriculture, transmitted to the managers by Sir Joseph Banks (Berman, 1978, p.55.) Leather was a key product at the time, used wherever a strong but flexible material was required. As a rural industry that drew heavily on landowners' resources, tanning is hardly a surprising interest for improving landlords. A dwindling indigenous supply of oak trees – from the bark of which tannin, the principal tanning chemical, was traditionally derived – coupled with war and blockade meant that the raw materials for the tanning process were in short supply. Davy developed a straightforward test which tanners could use to determine the quality of tannin derived from whatever sources they could find. As part of the investigations, Sir Joseph Banks asked Davy to test a potential foreign substitute for oak bark, hoping to open up a new product line for the East India Company. This is another example of Banks using his network of non-governmental bodies to link science to the service of the state, which you saw in Units 12–13 (Gascoigne, 1998, p.129).

Davy's lectures were well received and formed the basis of a paper which would be the definitive work on tanning for another 50 years. Furthermore, this work added lustre to Davy's growing reputation, for he received on account of it the first of what would be his many public awards, the Copley Medal of the Royal Society, of which Banks was president at the time.

'A discourse introductory to a course of lectures on chemistry', 1802

As had been the case in his first season at the RI, Davy gave more than just the series of lectures on tanning during the 1801–2 season. In January 1802 he began a series on chemistry with 'A discourse introductory to a course of lectures on chemistry'. Coleridge was in the audience. The text of this lecture is reproduced in full in Anthology II. This has become one of the most famous lectures in the history of science. It was a manifesto both for Davy the 'campaigner' (his word) for science and for the Royal Institution. When first delivered, it had a bigger impact than even Davy anticipated:

> I am induced to publish the following discourse in consequence of the request of a part of the audience before whom it was delivered, the accuracy of whose judgment it would be presumptuous in me to question. It was not originally intended for the press. The subject is too important and sublime to be justly treated in an occasional composition; and the views I have taken were designed rather to excite feelings of interest concerning it, than to give minute information.
>
> 26 April 1802
>
> Humphry Davy
>
> (Davy, 1839a, p.310)

EXERCISE To me, this reads as a genuine concern about publishing rather than as false modesty.

1 Why do you think Davy might have been reluctant to publish both as an author and as a natural philosopher?

2 What do you think Davy meant by the term 'sublime' here?

DISCUSSION 1 As we have seen, Davy was a careful author, who was aware that writing was the permanent, and most important, means of communicating his scientific work. The tone and rhetorical style of a lecture would be very different than a written piece planned as such. The introductory lecture was 'to excite feelings', as contrasted with a written piece, which required 'minute information'. The answer from the perspective of the natural philosopher is much the same: proper written presentation of natural philosophy involved a style distinct from that of a spoken lecture.

2 Davy seems to be using 'sublime' here in the sense of 'elevated' or 'awesome', a subject which would indeed excite feelings. The idea of the sublime was developed in Units 16 and 17.

The 'introductory discourse' appeared in print in April 1802, and thus reached a much wider audience than would have been the case had it been experienced by only a single group of listeners. Introducing the discourse in his edition of his brother's *Collected Works*, John Davy explained his selection:

> In point of time, they [the introductory lecture and the syllabus of lectures of which it formed part] belong to his early productions; and are as characteristic of his scientific youth, with its enthusiasm and vigor, as his essays were of his infancy in science. – Designed by him for an audience supposed to be ignorant of chemistry; and yet enlightened and refined, for the purpose of rousing attention, and exciting an interest, and giving elementary knowledge, they appear well adapted to answer the same purposes to readers of a similar class ... To chemical readers it is hoped, they may not be unacceptable, as historical sketches of the then state of the science.
>
> (Davy, 1839a, p.308)

Almost exactly 200 years later as I write, we are just the sort of audience that Davy had in mind. His audience at the RI would have heard the lecture in one sitting of probably some 90 minutes duration, but with the benefit of Davy's animated delivery. It would have been the sheer force of Davy's personality as a lecturer that held the audience. Chemical demonstrations, 'stinks and bangs', were a great attraction for the RI's audience. As one commentator said: 'They [the other sciences] are not susceptible of any brilliant exhibitions; there is no noise, no fire ...' (quoted in Foote, 1952, p.11). However, this introductory lecture had none. Contemporary readers of the written version, unlike the listeners, could have suited their own convenience, reading it either as a whole or in sections. Though printed without any section headings or breaks, it falls into a number of sections. As part of your task is to become accustomed to the early nineteenth-century style of Davy's rhetoric, we will study it section by section. For convenience of reference, I have added paragraph numbers to the original.

EXERCISE Now read paragraphs 1–4, which define chemistry, and paragraphs 5–11, which discuss its relationship to the other sciences (Anthology II, pp.148–51). Then answer the following question:

Why was chemistry the key science of the period, according to Davy?

DISCUSSION Chemistry deals with all material substances 'found upon our globe', their changes and interactions from the most minute scale to the grandest. Therefore, all other sciences are dependent upon it for knowledge of the specific properties of bodies: mechanical philosophy; natural history, including mineralogy, botany and zoology; the medical sciences of medicine, physiology and pharmacy; and even (tenuously) astronomy. Not only does it provide facts needed by the other sciences, it also provides tools ('instruments and powers of investigation'): 'the most powerful and useful of his [the mechanical philosopher's] agents', analytical methods for mineralogists, the material constituents of the astronomer's tools.

However, in paragraph 11, showing the influence of the Bristol circle and associationist psychology, Davy argues for the unity of scientific knowledge and against specialization because 'for man, all the different parts of the human mind are possessed of certain harmonious relations' (Fullmer, 2000, pp.122, 157–8). As all of the sciences 'consist of expressions of facts more or less analogous', they must be interconnected. 'The man of true genius' should not be limited by artificial boundaries of definition, but 'pursue the plans of his own mind' to combine whatever knowledge is necessary in pursuit of discovery, connecting facts by 'simple and obvious analogies' (see Units 16 and 17 on the idea of genius). Here Davy is explicitly applying associationist ideas.

After defining chemistry and arguing that it is on a par with the established sciences, Davy turns in paragraphs 12–18 to an aspect of chemistry that was fundamental to winning support from his RI audiences: its applications 'to most of the processes and operations of common life'. Not only does chemistry provide necessities, but it is also the source of the 'most refined enjoyments and delicate pleasures of civilized society'. In this regard, he points out in paragraph 4, the study of chemistry is particularly timely because new instruments were available to enhance its applications.

EXERCISE

Now read paragraphs 12–18. Then answer the following questions:

1 What is the specific utility of chemistry to each of the areas of application?

2 What is the underlying motive for applying chemistry in these ways?

DISCUSSION

1 Agriculture – the application of chemistry will lead to higher agricultural productivity.
Metallurgy ('the working of metals') – this *is* a branch of technical chemistry.
Bleaching and dyeing – these are of their nature chemical processes. The application of chemical theory to dyeing will lead to new permanent, artificial colours.
Tanning – this important industry has been systematized and improved (by Davy's work).
Porcelain and glass – Davy does not say how chemistry is relevant to the production of porcelain and glass, but rather assumes it.

2 Underlying Davy's discussion is the Enlightenment motive of improvement by means of the application of science.

What better justification could there be for studying chemistry than that given in paragraph 18? Everything depends on chemistry: 'it is difficult to examine any of our common operations or labours without finding them more or less connected with chemistry'. Notice also the human aspects of the applications of science. Through scientific knowledge, the status of the agriculturist will be enhanced. Metallurgy, however, provides double-edged swords that can be used for good or ill, so that it is difficult 'to ascertain the effects of this art upon the progress of the human mind'. It is the habits and fashions of society which make dyeing an important area of chemical application. Human inventions are required on the part of the artist to solve the problem of the tendency of natural dyes to fade by substituting new, permanent colours. Furthermore, in the case of tanning, taking advantage of scientific improvements requires of workmen new attitudes towards innovation; the chemical philosopher is limited in his influence. Thus while Davy sees chemistry as fundamental to improvement, he is not a determinist. For Davy, there is no automatic path from discovery to application; he argues for the importance of human agency in the interactions between science and its application.

EXERCISE Turning to the language of paragraph 18, what imagery is used to convey man's relationship with nature? How is nature portrayed?

DISCUSSION It is very much *man's* relationship with nature that concerns Davy here (despite his large female audience). Note that it is a power relationship. Nature is depicted as female. Man 'employed ... substances in nature' for his 'satisfaction' or 'gratification'. Man penetrates nature's depths to allay 'the restlessness of his desires' or extend and increase his power. Man is 'to a certain extent ruler' of the elements. He can subject 'to his purposes' heat and light, which under his control become 'instruments of comfort and enjoyment, or of terror and destruction.'

In paragraphs 19–22, Davy suggests that to study the history of the development of chemistry is to study the history of the progressive improvement of society. Scientific knowledge gives man 'mastery' of nature, and progress through science will continue: 'we may reasonably look forward to a state of greater cultivation and happiness than that we at present enjoy.' You might like to recall these points when studying Goethe's *Faust* in Units 26–27.

EXERCISE Now read paragraphs 23–7. Then answer the following question:

What are Davy's scientific aims?

DISCUSSION In paragraph 23 Davy expresses a desire to move chemical philosophy on from being a collection of facts to the discovery of general laws in order to understand man's physical and moral constitution.

Notice his stress in paragraph 27 on the importance of communicating science by means of print. Once written down, 'true philosophy will never be despised; the germs of improvement are sown in minds even where they are not perceived, and sooner or later the spring-time of their growth must arrive.' He presents an image of chemistry as a progressive science that will lead to the improvement of not just the arts but society. However, Davy's vision of the role of science in society is not of radical challenge to the established order like Priestley's.

EXERCISE Read paragraph 28 and describe Davy's view of the political and social roles of science. 'Projectors' as used in this paragraph refer to people promoting projects.

DISCUSSION Davy sees scientific knowledge as greasing the wheels of the current system. By patronizing science, the wealthy will be in a position to better discharge their duties to the poor. Social inequalities are the drivers of social change, but such change need not be revolutionary. Scientific knowledge is the means by which the whole of society will move in an orderly manner towards improvement.

Davy sees a meliorative role for scientific knowledge, which resonates with the discussion of New Lanark in Units 18–19. This is a vision of Enlightenment improvement in the service of the established, but not stagnant, social order. It is an appropriate message for his audience at the Royal Institution, still worried about what had happened in France. They were not opposed to change but wanted to be in control of it. Change, Davy argues, is within their grasp. Paragraph 28 concludes with the ringing sentences: 'We consider only a state of human progression arising out of its present condition. We look for a time that we may reasonably expect, for a bright day of which we already behold the dawn.'

However, in Davy's view it is not only for economic and social improvement that chemistry is valuable.

EXERCISE Paragraphs 30–4 discuss the intellectual value of science. Read these paragraphs now and summarize Davy's views.

DISCUSSION Science enhances pleasure because it is a stimulant to mental activity and new ideas (30). It is a natural human mental process to be engaged by objects and phenomena that are to hand and to consider their inter-relationships. This process of engagement trains the mental faculties (31). Furthermore, the study of nature engages the aesthetic sensibilities and through its indefiniteness constantly stimulates the soul (32), an echo of the discussion of Lake District aesthetics in Units 16 and 17. In particular, the study of chemistry and the physical sciences may stimulate the jaded sophisticate without harming others (33). Experimental research expands the minds of men of business or mechanical employment, while it consoles the jaded fashionable classes and prevents intellectuals having fanciful notions. Finally, the study of science reveals 'in all the phenomena of the universe the designs of a perfect intelligence' (34).

Thus as well as presenting chemistry as an agent of improvement towards the 'bright day', Davy also provides an argument for science as liberal education, a stimulus to 'mental activity' and 'new ideas' that engages 'the aesthetic sensibilities'. Here Davy combines Enlightenment and Romantic thinking.

EXERCISE What view of the relations between science and religion does paragraph 34 suggest that Davy held?

DISCUSSION The final sentence suggests that Davy advocated natural theology, the view that the study of nature and nature's laws revealed the wisdom of God.

The final sentence was probably the most reassuring of all to Davy's audience. Because the designs of a perfect intelligence in the universe were demonstrated to them, students of experimental philosophy 'will uniformly appear as the friend of tranquility and order'. In paragraph 33, he argues that the sciences provide evidence of simplicity of design in nature and demonstrated that 'every being is intended for some definite end or purpose'. Natural theology made it possible for science to reveal harmony and stability in the natural world. Chemistry would preserve both the social order and religious orthodoxy while guaranteeing progress towards the 'bright day' (Golinski, 1992, p.198). On the eve of the Treaty of Amiens with Napoleon's France, which everyone hoped would prove permanent, this optimistic message from the young and earnest Davy thrilled his audience. His series of lectures on chemistry was a resounding success both for Davy personally and for the Royal Institution to which he attracted new subscribers. He had turned a radical, threatening chemistry into reassuring, polite knowledge: that is, knowledge for its own sake seen as a cultural acquisition.

EXERCISE If you have time, at this point read through Davy's lecture in one sitting in order to get a feel for its shape and the flow of Davy's rhetoric.

After Davy's death, a friend commented to his first biographer about the first series of chemical lectures:

> Men of the first rank and talent, – the literary and the scientific, the practical and the theoretical, blue-stockings, and women of fashion, the old and the young, all crowded – eagerly crowded the lecture-room. His youth, his simplicity, his natural eloquence, his chemical knowledge, his happy illustrations and well-

conducted experiments, excited universal attention and unbounded applause. Compliments, invitations and presents, were showered upon him in abundance from all quarters; his society was coveted by all, and all appeared proud of his acquaintance.

(Quoted in Treneer, 1963, p.86)

5 Professor of Chemistry at the Royal Institution, 1802–12

The end of pneumatic chemistry

Davy was promoted to Professor of Chemistry in May 1802, an eventful month in the RI's history. For in that same month James Gillray published a famous, unflattering caricature of a demonstration of nitrous oxide there (see Plate 20.3, *Scientific Researches! – New Discoveries in Pneumaticks! – or an Experimental Lecture on the Powers of Air*). It is tempting to associate the caricature with the event two years earlier described in the quotation above from Lady Holland (p.36). The gentleman inhaling the gas has been identified as Sir John Coxe Hippisley, whose 'performance' she had recorded. However, Davy, whom Gillray shows holding a pair of bellows, was not yet at the RI when it occurred. A number of RI managers are in the audience. Whether Hippisley subjected himself more than once to such a public display (as contrasted with private inhalation) is a matter of conjecture rather than historical record. The etching was made during the period when Gillray, influenced by Burke (as were a number of other satirists), received an annual pension from the Tory government and was generally anti-Whig in his sympathies. Some have read the cartoon as a satire on the politics of Count Rumford, who wanted to use the RI not just for the scientific education of the elite, but also for that of artisans and 'mechanics', a programme which many saw as too radical (Fullmer, 1960, p.12). On this reading, the scene is a reference to the radical associations of pneumatic chemistry. For example, there are several references to Lavoisierian, 'French' chemistry, including the frog under the jar on the right-hand side of the demonstation bench. On one level, it is related to air pump experiments, but on another it was already at this time a pejorative reference to the French.

Rumford is the figure standing on the far right. Indeed, the timing of the publication in the same month that Rumford left the RI and England for good to take up residence in France, together with the fact that Hippisley (the person being made a fool of and whom Rumford is laughing at) was the RI's treasurer, suggests a further interpretative layer. There was a view circulating privately among the RI's managers during the spring of 1802 that Rumford had embezzled considerable amounts of RI funds over the previous year, under Hippisley's nose as it were (Berman, 1978, pp.29–30; Chilton and Coley, 1980, p.175). Gillray may well have been commenting on that as well as questioning an enterprise under such leadership.

Though Davy was still in Bristol at the time of the incident recorded by Lady Holland, as we noted above, he did demonstrate the effects of nitrous oxide at the RI a year later: that is, a year before the cartoon was published. Hippisley was a friend and patron of Davy. However, Davy's appearance in this cartoon may have been simply a mischievous addition by Gillray to the earlier incident, suggesting perhaps that the new professor's published researches had an unscientific side to them, a not uncommon view as we have seen.

EXERCISE Compare Plate 20.3 (1802) with Plate 20.4 (1803) and answer the following questions:

1 In what ways do the settings differ?

2 How is Davy represented in each?

DISCUSSION

1 The Gillray caricature is set during a demonstration in the public lecture theatre of the Royal Institution with Davy at the demonstration bench. The portrait is set in a vague but undoubtedly more private space with Davy seated at a writing table.

2 Gillray represents Davy as a rather mischievous showman of science who is not averse to being involved in discomfiting the public with scientific demonstrations. The Howard portrait a year later shows Davy in thoughtful pose as a serious, contemplative natural philosopher. The portrait, in the production of which he presumably collaborated, showed Davy in a far more favourable light than the cartoon, as if he had 'moved on'.

Golinski (1992, p.201) has suggested that chemistry and Davy's own activities being lampooned so publicly may have resulted in his abandoning public experimental demonstrations of nitrous oxide. Apparently, they ceased not long after the cartoon was published. However, we have seen that Davy had already left nitrous oxide behind as a research area before moving to London. Having reached his goal of the professorship, Davy may well have been ready to leave behind the 'shows' as well. Demonstrations of the effects of nitrous oxide were rather unpredictable and uncontrollable, so their value as entertainment threatened to undermine the goal of the display of rational, useful science. Davy continued to be a showman and to attract huge audiences to the RI, but he put the radical science of the Bristol years, and the potential opprobrium, behind him.

Agricultural chemistry

In any case, also in May 1802, the direction of Davy's next set of researches was decided by the Board of Agriculture's request that he give a series of lectures on the applications of chemistry to agriculture, a characteristic Enlightenment programme. Several proprietors and active managers of the RI were improving landlords who also belonged to the Board, which was therefore influential in running the RI in its early years. As Davy had suggested in his 'Discourse', the application of chemistry held out the promise of higher crop yields that would in turn bring higher profits, but it also held out the prospect of sufficient food for the rapidly increasing population and would therefore serve to avert social disaster. To prepare for this lecture series, which was first held in the spring of 1803 and then annually until 1812, Davy visited farmers, analyzed soils, studied the chemical effects of manures, and performed experiments and trials on great estates. From this time onwards, Davy regularly undertook agricultural analyses at the RI, and also at a laboratory built for him nearby at the Board of Agriculture. The lectures on agricultural chemistry, too, were very successful. Davy acquired an additional appointment (and salary) as Professor of Chemical Agriculture to the Board.

These lectures were not published until 1813, after Davy had left the RI. His *Agricultural Chemistry* remained the standard work in the field until the 1840s. As with the work on the chemistry of tanning, Davy's achievement was to describe good practice rather than to contribute chemically based innovation to agriculture. One of the outcomes of Davy's agricultural work, as had been the case with tanning, was a set of standard tests for the analysis of soils which could be carried out by the farmer using an inexpensive field kit. Every farmer could be his own analyst, though just how straightforward the farmers of the day would have found the procedures is open to question.

In the first lecture of the published work, Davy made clear his Baconian view of scientific method:

> Nothing is more wanting in agriculture than experiments in which all the circumstances are minutely and scientifically detailed. ...
>
> Information collected after views of distinct inquiry would necessarily be fitted for inductive reasoning, and capable of being connected with the general principles of science; and a few histories of the results of truly philosophical experiments in agricultural chemistry would be of more value in enlightening

> and benefiting the farmer, than the greatest possible accumulation of imperfect trials, conducted merely in the empirical spirit.
>
> (Davy, 1840, p.195)

For Davy, his work on agricultural chemistry was not only a matter of science but also a route for his own social progress. The first lecture flattered and reassured his landowning audience in terms similar to those expressed in his 'Discourse'. However, his social confidence had grown to the point where he felt able to chivvy them as well:

> It is from the higher classes of the community, from the proprietors of land, – those who are fitted by their education to form enlightened plans, and, by their fortunes, to carry such plans into execution: it is from these that the principles of improvement must flow to the labouring classes of the community; and in all classes the benefit is mutual; for the interest of the tenantry must be always likewise the interests of the proprietors of the soil. The attention of the labourer will be more minute, and he will exert himself more for improvement, when he is certain he cannot deceive his employer, and has a conviction of the extent of his knowledge. Ignorance in the possessor of an estate, of the manner in which it ought to be treated, generally leads either to inattention or injudicious practices in the tenant or bailiff.
>
> (Davy, 1840, p.197)

Davy's work for the improving landlords of the Board of Agriculture brought him increasingly into association with the ruling classes. Plate 20.5 shows Davy at a sheep shearing on the Duke of Bedford's estate. The sixth Duke, like the fifth Duke before him, was the very model of the improving landlord. In collaboration with the estate's head gardener, George Sinclair, Davy performed there a series of scientific trials of different kind of grasses, a summary of which was included in his *Agricultural Chemistry*. This painting of 1804 by George Garrard, a Royal Academy-trained painter of animal scenes and modeller of prize animals who enjoyed patronage from Bedfordshire landowners, was a study for an engraving which the ever hard-up Garrard produced for sale to those who were present at the gathering (Carter, 1979, p.583).[3] Garrard himself

[3] The central column, in front of which we see the mounted sixth Duke of Bedford, was an artistic invention. The plinth at the base of the column has the inscription 'science' while that at the top has the inscription 'technology'; together they represent the Enlightenment view that technology rests on science and results in the prosperity exemplified by the people gathered at the sheep shearing, The column did not appear in the final engraving. The sheep shearings were annual events for transacting agricultural business as well as promoting the latest agricultural techniques.

can be seen in the lower left-hand corner with some of his models. Davy is shown in a group on the right-hand side of the painting, listening to the famous innovative agriculturalist T.W. Coke in the company of Board of Agriculture members Sir Joseph Banks (seated), Sir John Sinclair and Arthur Young. Davy became a regular attender at such events and was part of the country-house social circle of several great estates. To be sure, the fact that Davy was genuinely a sportsman – both knowledgeable and capable from his Cornish days – as well as a noted raconteur would have made him a welcome visitor.

Fellow of the Royal Society

For his work on the chemistry of tanning, Davy was made a Fellow of the Royal Society in 1803, the year in which the work by the popular portrait painter Henry Howard was exhibited at the Royal Academy (see Plate 20.4).[4] This was the same year that Davy started his lectures on agricultural chemistry. Whether intentionally or not, the portrait would have worked as a riposte to the unfortunate image of Davy in the Gillray cartoon. At the Royal Academy, it would have been on show to the same sort of audience as he addressed at the RI. Here is a modestly dressed, confident, certainly respectable young professor, already famous and on the verge of great achievement.

EXERCISE Look carefully at Plate 20.4.

1 Why might it be called a chemical portrait?

2 What aspect of Davy's work is stressed?

3 You may have noticed that I used the term 'natural philosopher' rather than 'scientist' to characterize Davy in the second answer to the previous exercise (p.48). Refer back to Units 12–13, p.90. Why is 'natural philosopher' the more appropriate term?

DISCUSSION 1 There is chemical glassware on a shelf over Davy's right shoulder. If you have some experience of laboratory science, perhaps from school, you might also have mentioned that on the table are pen and notebooks for (perhaps) laboratory or lecture notes.

2 The emphasis is on Davy as a writer. It is the writing up of his chemical experiments which is stressed here. Chemical apparatus is in the background.

[4] It is unclear who commissioned the portrait and the whereabouts of the original are unknown, though the copy now at the National Portrait Gallery was at one time in the collection of Davy's close Bristol friend and colleague at the Pneumatic Institution, Dr John King.

3 As Units 12–13 point out, 'natural philosopher' was used at the time for people we would now call 'scientists'. Strictly, it would be anachronistic to refer to Davy as a 'scientist'.

However popular and famous – perhaps even notorious, as Gillray made out – Davy's lectures were, it was in fact through his writings that most people became acquainted with his scientific work. That is, it was through his published writings that he drew out of notebooks of the type shown here. Every historian who has ever worked on Davy's notebooks comments on their chaotic organization. Davy would start from both ends at different times, and then mix laboratory notes with stray drafts of poems and personal matters as if he did not want to lose a single thought. Indeed, some of the jottings from his earliest Penzance notebooks found their way into his final work, which was published posthumously (Knight, 1992, p.17). It was through the interaction between his lecturing and his writing that Davy's chemical researches, his experiments, became public science.

Davy is a very early British example of an individual earning a living by means of scientific research, but to call him a 'scientist' in 1803 is to put too modern a spin on his outlook. Davy was not concerned primarily to pursue specialist knowledge in a particular field. He saw himself as a chemical philosopher developing a world view within a tradition of natural theology, using science to establish the existence and beneficence of God (Knight, 1992, p.5). In fact, the way that Davy constructed his own scientific career contributed to the creation of the role or identity of professional 'scientist', which was legitimated by the neologism in the decade after his death. In this respect, Davy represented the beginning of a change; he should not be viewed as a result of it. How confident Davy himself was of his prospects along this career path and how confident he was in the early 1800s of the future of the RI are both open to question. Despite his successes in the lecture theatre and his rapid assimilation by polite society, Davy clearly still had thoughts that a more traditional professional career might be a preferable path. In 1804 he registered to follow a medical course at Jesus College, Cambridge, perhaps as a form of insurance; he never took it up.

The laboratory reorganized

In April 1803 plans were put in train to reorganize the RI's laboratory provision (Berman, 1978, p.28). In one respect, this was made possible by Rumford's departure and the consequent release of space that the fulfilment of certain of his institutional aims would have required. On a practical level, preparations for the elaborate lecture demonstrations were crowding the available research facilities; separate preparative and research spaces were desirable. Additionally, the letter from Davy to his friend John King, quoted above (p.39), points to a further level of scientific activity – private demonstrations to select gatherings of natural philosophers and proprietors of the RI. Space for that too was to be created. It was not until 1804 that the full reorganization was accomplished with the knocking through of a wall in what would be the basement research laboratory to create a linked small lecture theatre that would seat some 120. Not only would this give chosen members privileged direct access to whatever Davy wanted to show them, but also it would give Davy an audience for his research work. That is, it would bring together people who could provide testimony, much as his experimental subjects with nitrous oxide had. In this case, they did not participate in the work, but they witnessed it. This was the site not of spectacular demonstrations for dramatic effect, but of the detailed unfolding of an experimental strategy in an inner sanctum. This strategy in turn encouraged increased financial support for his work (Golinski, 1992, pp.220–1).

EXERCISE Now study the Royal Institution on the 'Sites of science' section of the CD-ROM or in the Activities Booklet (ALE 7).

Scientific researches

The first Bakerian lecture – the electrolysis of water

Once the lectures on agricultural chemistry were established and circumstances at the Royal Institution were more stable, Davy resumed researches on electrochemistry in the autumn of 1806, producing a brilliant series of results which would be presented in the Bakerian lectures of 1806 and 1807. The annual Bakerian lecture was an endowed lectureship in the gift of the Royal Society. Therefore, Davy's immediate audience would have been scientifically sophisticated, though the publication of the lectures made possible a wider readership. It was a great honour to be invited to present one. Davy gave five in all. The first two in particular would secure his enduring fame.

Davy's chief tool was a Voltaic battery with 100 pairs of plates of the kind with which he had already worked while still in Bristol. Indeed, Fullmer (2000, p.3) argues that these two famous lectures, produced when he was not yet 30, were in fact synthetic works in which Davy drew together several strands of his researches thus far. The specific motive for Davy's return to Voltaic work is unclear. Golinski suggests that publications of 1805 and 1806 which argued that the Voltaic battery was a synthetic tool – that new substances could be created from water by electrolysis – may have motivated Davy to defend his earlier work establishing it as an analytical tool. Whatever the stimulus, he returned to the question of the electrolysis of water and, by means of painstaking experiments to eliminate impurities and side reactions, proved that water was indeed separated by electrolysis exclusively into hydrogen and oxygen in precise proportions by volume. At the same time, he was limiting the possibilities of contradiction by chemists with other views, and he clinched the effectiveness of the Voltaic battery as an instrument. He raised the scientific stakes. Much as had been the case with Lavoisier's experiments, future investigators of the problem would have to have the resources to be able to operate with the same equipment as Davy, or rely upon his demonstrations (Golinski, 1992, pp.209–12).

More important than his determination of the facts of the case were his conclusions about the electrical nature of matter. He could not explain the mechanism of electrochemical action and recognized that there were a number of plausible hypotheses, but he was reluctant to theorize:

> Amongst the substances that combine chemically, all those, the electrical energies of which are well known, exhibit opposite states ... supposing perfect freedom of motion in their particles or elementary matter, they ought, according to the principles laid down, to attract each other in consequence of their electrical powers. In the present state of our knowledge, it would be useless to attempt to speculate on the remote cause of the electrical energy, or the reason why different bodies, after being brought into contact, should be found differently electrified; its relation to chemical affinity is, however, evident. May it not be identical with it, and an essential property of matter?
>
> (Quoted in Knight, 1992, pp.63–4)

With this statement, Davy effectively launched the science of electrochemistry, bringing together the study of electricity and the study of chemistry. It was a dynamical science of forces, energies and powers along a Newtonian line of attractions between particles rather than a static, materialistic chemistry of starting materials and end products with no attention to the nature of chemical change. Having begun this research in August, he delivered it as a Bakerian lecture to the Royal Society in November 1806, and it was published in the following year.

EXERCISE Now study the first Bakerian lecture (Electrolysis of water) on the 'Dictionary of chemistry' section of the CD-ROM or in the Activities Booklet (ALE 8).

In 1807 Davy was awarded a prize of the First Class of the Institute of France for his researches on electricity reported in the first Bakerian lecture. This prize had been instituted in the summer of 1802. By way of inducement to undertake electrical researches, Napoleon had announced a substantial financial prize for the French or foreign experimenter who advanced 'electricity and galvanism to a degree comparable to the advances made in these sciences by Franklin [in America] and Volta' (quoted in Crosland, 1967, p.21). The commission of the Institute, which administered the electrical prize, decided to award smaller, annual prizes until such time as a truly epochal electrical discovery merited the full award. Davy's prize in 1807 was the second annual award.

The second Bakerian lecture – the isolation of new elements

Having thus established the efficacy of the Voltaic battery as a tool, a year later Davy gave a second Bakerian lecture in which he announced that he had used a battery with 250 pairs of plates to discover two new elementary substances, sodium and potassium. He isolated these from the well-known alkalis soda and potash, which were fundamental to many processes of applied chemistry. Again, Davy was challenging Lavoisier, for the new elements were additions to Lavoisier's list of elementary substances. Their isolation was not the only issue, for the two new substances exhibited puzzling properties. Davy correctly classified them as metals on the basis of their having properties analogous to those of other metals. This provides another example of his use of associationist methodology:

> Should these bases of potash and soda be called metals? The greater number of philosophical persons to whom this question has been put, have answered in the affirmative. They agree with metals in opacity, lustre, malleability, conducting powers as to heat and electricity, and in their qualities of chemical combination ... and in the philosophical division of the classes of bodies, the analogy between the greater number of properties must always be the foundation of arrangement.
>
> (Quoted in Knight, 1992, p.67)

EXERCISE Now study the second Bakerian lecture (Isolation of new elements) on the 'Dictionary of chemistry' section of the CD-ROM or in the Activities Booklet (ALE 9).

Extending this work in 1808, Davy isolated the alkaline earth elements barium, strontium and magnesium from substances which Lavoisier had thought to be elementary already – a total of five new elements in less than a year. However, he had unknowingly been anticipated by Berzelius, the great Swedish chemist, with regard to the discovery of the last three.

When it was pointed out to Napoleon by Davy's French chemical contemporaries that to surpass Davy's achievements a more powerful battery than that of the Royal Institution would be needed, the emperor would not let France be outdone:

> His Imperial Majesty in the middle of his concern for the affairs of state does not ignore any important progress in science and does not refuse to the sciences anything that might contribute to further success. He ordered that there should be constructed at the École Polytechnique [in Paris] Voltaic piles of different sizes including one which should be bigger than any used hitherto.
>
> (Report of the secretary of the First Class of the Institute, 1808; quoted in Crosland, 1967, p.24)

By February 1808 funding for a French battery with 600 pairs of 30-centimetre-square plates was authorized, and it was in use by July (see Figure 20.7). Davy in turn used this French commitment to advantage to win funding for an even bigger battery for the RI. He wrote to the managers in July 1808:

Figure 20.7 Anonymous, The Powerful Voltaic Battery Constructed at the Polytechnic Institute in Paris in 1808 by Order of Napoleon, *in Louis Figuier,* Les Merveilles de la science, ou description populaire des inventions modernes, *6 vols, 1867. Photo: Burndy Library, Dibner Institute for the History of Science and Technology, Cambridge, Massachusetts.*

Probably not very accurate, this image was first published in 1867 as France under Napoleon III was flexing its scientific and technical muscles after the Austro-Prussian War of 1866 in anticipation of a possible conflict with Prussia, which did in fact come about in the Franco-Prussian War of 1870–1. It is another example of the science of the era of Napoleon I being invoked for purposes of prestige and propaganda.

> A new path of discovery having been opened in the agencies of the electrical battery of Volta, which promises to lead to the greatest improvements in Chemistry and Natural Philosophy, and the useful arts connected with them; and since the increase of the size of the apparatus is absolutely necessary for pursuing it to its full extent, it is proposed to raise a fund by subscription, for constructing a powerful battery, worthy of a national establishment, and capable of promoting the great objects of science. Already, in other countries, public and ample means have been provided for pursuing these investigations. They have had their origin in this country; and it would be dishonourable to a nation so great, so powerful, and so rich, if, from the want of pecuniary resources, they should be completed abroad. An appeal to enlightened individuals on this subject can scarcely be made in vain. It is proposed that the instrument and apparatus be erected in the Laboratory of the Royal Institution, where it shall be employed in the advancement of this new department of science.
>
> (Quoted in Knight, 1992, p.84)

EXERCISE What strategies did Davy use to make his case?

DISCUSSION Davy appealed to the Enlightenment spirit of voluntary, private patronage for worthy ends. He invoked national prestige, competitive advantage with respect to other countries (indeed one with which Britain was at war) and the desire not to lose out in the development phase on work that was initiated in Britain. He also appealed to the managers' self-image as enlightened individuals and mentioned that the new battery might result in useful applications.

The result was a £1,000 fund which allowed the construction of a battery made of 2,000 eight-inch (20-centimetre) square double-plates, the most powerful in the world at the time. It was inaugurated in 1809. For Davy, making science public involved well-funded, privately supported central institutions and the audiences that they entailed. In turn, having privileged access to such facilities came to define science.

The fifth Bakerian Lecture – chlorine

The scientific rivalry with Davy's great French contemporaries was intense. His brother likened it to the military campaigns that were occupying the chemists' two nations on a different front. A particular area of confrontation was the elementary nature of oxymuriatic acid, a substance which, on Lavoisier's theory, was supposed to combine with oxygen to give muriatic acid. In this case, alongside chemical tests, Davy used the Voltaic pile negatively to show that oxymuriatic acid could not be further broken down and was therefore another chemical element, which he named chlorine. This new element behaved rather like oxygen in terms of the substances with which it combined, and it was found that there was no oxygen in muriatic acid, another challenge to Lavoisier's thinking. Davy dealt with this problem in his fifth Bakerian lecture in 1810, and he made his antipathy to French chemistry clear. However, it took a long time for these results to be accepted generally in the chemical community.

> Oxymuriatic acid gas is not an acid, any more than oxygen; but it becomes acid, like that substance, by combining with inflammable matter [hydrogen] ... The confidence of the French enquirers closed for nearly a century this noble path of investigation which I have endeavoured to exhibit to you. Nothing is so fatal to the progress of the human mind as to suppose that our views of science are ultimate; that there are no mysteries in nature; that our triumphs are complete, and that there are no new worlds to conquer.
>
> (Quoted in Knight, 1992, p.87)

The unity of matter

All of this electrolytic work confirmed for Davy that chemical composition was not the key to understanding the behaviour of substances, but rather that natural philosophy should look to the force and powers associated with matter for explanations. That is, Davy rejected the static chemistry of substances of Priestley and Lavoisier and embraced a dynamical chemistry, following Newton in developing a model of attractive forces between particles (Knight, 1992, pp.63–4). Furthermore, the isolation of so many new elements conflicted with Davy's belief in an underlying unity of matter. He disagreed with the Mancunian chemist John Dalton's now classical view published in 1807 that the smallest particle of a chemical element, which retained all the properties of that element, was an atom. On that view, there were as many distinct kinds of atom as there were elements. This did not accord with Davy's view of the essential simplicity of nature. He rejected Dalton's chemical atomic theory, favouring instead Newton's view that one type of physical particle – the atom – was the basic constituent of all matter, with distinct chemical substances being the result of their arrangement, or perhaps differing electrical states. Davy also entertained the alternative view that the atom was not a physical entity at all, but rather a concentration of forces at a particular point. Such views were not held by the majority of chemists at the time (Brock, 1992, chs 3 and 4).

So convinced was he of the underlying unity of matter that he argued that the elements, defined in the laboratory in Lavoisierian terms as substances which could be broken down no further by chemical analysis, might themselves be 'compound' substances. He thought that they might still be broken down by an as yet undiscovered analytical tool even more powerful than the Voltaic battery. That nature should be simple, harmonious and intelligible was, for Davy, the design of a beneficient Creator, as he argued in 1812:

> A few undecompounded bodies, which may, perhaps, ultimately be resolved into still fewer elements, or which may be different forms of the same material, constitute the whole of our tangible universe of things. By experiment they are discovered ... and experiment is as it were, the chain that binds down the Proteus of nature, and obliges it to confess its real form and divine nature. The laws which govern the phenomena of chemistry produce invariable results; which may be made the guide of operations in the arts; and which ensure the uniformity of the system of nature, the arrangements of which are marked by creative intelligence, and made constantly subservient to the production of life, and the increase of happiness.
>
> (Quoted in Knight, 1992, p.78)

6 Mrs Marcet's *Conversations on Chemistry*

Jane Marcet, the writer

It was not only through his lectures and his own publications that Davy's chemistry was brought to the public. In 1806 there appeared a two-volume work entitled *Conversations on Chemistry*. Anonymously authored by a woman, the book became immensely popular, going through 16 British editions (with 23 impressions) up to 1853, two French, one Swiss, one German and 23 US editions (with possibly as many as 160 impressions). No British edition had a print run of fewer than 1,000 copies; the tenth edition, from which you will be reading extracts, had a print run of 2,000. According to records of her British publisher, Longman & Co, 20,000 copies altogether of British editions were printed, giving profits of some £46,000, which were divided evenly between author and publisher (Horrocks, 1987, pp.31, 78–9). Michael Faraday, Davy's associate and later successor as Professor of Chemistry at the RI, famously credited *Conversations on Chemistry,* which he read as a bookbinder's apprentice, with attracting him to the pursuit of science. Clearly, this was a successful book.

Figure 20.8 Anonymous, Jane Marcet, *c.1835–40, oil on canvas, 45 x 30 cm, private collection.*

It was not until the thirteenth edition in 1837 that the anonymous author's name, never really a secret, appeared on the title page; she was Mrs Jane Marcet (1769–1858) (see Figure 20.8). You have already met some of Mrs Marcet's chemical prose, for it is her text that the female voices are reading on the CD-ROM and that we have reproduced in the 'Dictionary of chemistry' section and in the ALE readings in Anthology II.

EXERCISE Now read the 'Preface' to *Conversations on Chemistry* (Anthology II, pp.158–60) and then answer the following questions:

1 Why was the book written and who is its intended audience?

2 What are the author's qualifications for writing such a text?

3 In what two ways does Mrs Marcet admit that she has 'cheated'?

DISCUSSION 1 The book was written to provide what we might call a foundation course in chemistry so that beginners, particularly females, could be brought up to speed sufficiently to be able to follow and derive benefit from the lecture demonstrations at the Royal Institution.

2 The author offers no qualifications for writing such a text except for 'conversing with a friend on the subject of chemistry, and of repeating a variety of experiments', plus having herself attended (and presumably read) the RI lectures.

3 First, to avoid repetition and asides for the sake of the flow of the book, she often includes remarks that were 'too acute for the young pupils, by whom they are supposed to be made'. Second, she has to assume a certain basic knowledge of natural philosophy on the part of her readers to make sense of the chemistry. Note that she eventually (in 1819) published *Conversations on Natural Philosophy* to deal with this deficiency, but did not alter subsequent editions, including ours of 1825, of the *Conversations on Chemistry.*

Jane Marcet (neé Haldimand) was the eldest child of a Swiss banker who married the daughter of an English silk merchant and manufacturer to whom young Haldimand had been sent as an apprentice. Haldimand's connections were good; he remained in England and his fortunes prospered. Unusual for England but common among Swiss patrician families, Jane and her sister enjoyed the same education from private tutors as her brothers, including such subjects as mathematics, astronomy and philosophy (Bahar, 2001, p.32). On her mother's death in 1783, she became mistress of the family home and hostess for her father's frequent social gatherings, which included bankers, politicians, writers, men of science and other intellectuals. She may well remind you of Mme de Staël, whom you met in Block 2. The family travelled widely and Jane also took art lessons from Sir Joshua Reynolds and Thomas Lawrence. Thus, she was well educated for a woman of the time, wealthy and well connected (Polkinghorn, 1993). In 1799 she married Dr Alexander Marcet (1770–1822), a Swiss immigrant who, fleeing political problems in his native Geneva, had taken his medical degree in Edinburgh and settled in London. They settled in the home of her father, for whom she retained her social duties.

Alexander Marcet introduced his wife to a new circle of scientific friends, for not only did he have a private medical practice, but he also lectured to medical students at Guys Hospital and was active in chemical research (as a private though relevant interest rather than in relation to his post). Among other things, he analyzed spring waters and promoted their therapeutic value, on which he hoped to turn a commercial profit. He was also heavily involved in promoting **vaccination** against smallpox (including of his and Jane's children) for both commercial and social reasons, stressing the benefits of medical science and hence practitioners (Bahar, 2001, pp.40–1). Alexander Marcet and his friends, mainly of the professional middle classes, typically belonged to newer scientific organizations such as the Medical and Chirurgical Society and the Geological Society. These tended to be outside of, indeed opposed to, the established Banksian scientific hierarchy. Those who later became members of the Royal Society tended to favour reforms. They also attended the Royal Institution and would later become active in its administration once the influence of powerful landowners within it declined (Horrocks, 1987, pp.14–25). Alexander Marcet, however, became a proprietor of the RI in 1801; both Marcets attended lectures at the RI, and Davy joined the guest list for Haldimand–Marcet soirées. Figure 20.9 shows the newly developed, fashionable Russell Square, an area occupied by the professional middle classes, to which the extended family moved from the village of Clapham in 1808.

Conversations on Chemistry was but the first of Jane Marcet's writing projects. She was independently wealthy and did not need to write for a living. However, she became a prolific author, especially after her final child was born. Indeed, after the death of Jane's father in 1819, the family enjoyed such inherited wealth that Alexander retired from medical practice and the family bought a considerable estate near Geneva to which they subsequently moved. However, the idyll was to be short-lived as Alexander died in 1822, so much of her writing was done in widowhood.

Conversations on Chemistry seems to have been motivated by genuine personal interest, as was her next major book, *Conversations on Political Economy*, which appeared in 1816, having been stimulated through her close friendship with the political economist David Ricardo and his family. It became the most widely read work in this field, which was a subject of considerable public debate at the time. Some subsequent topics were suggested by her publishers, who hoped for repeat successes. Above all, Jane Marcet had a genuine desire to educate, which she saw as a social responsibility – following on from the private responsibility for supervising the education of her younger siblings after her mother's death. She produced 'Conversations' on natural philosophy (1819), mineralogy (1822), evidences of Christianity (1826), vegetable physiology (1829), nature and art (1837), chronology (1837), land and water (1838), botany (1840), history of England part 1 (1842), part 2 (1844), language (1844), and harmony (1855). The 'Conversations' series was interspersed with 21 other works, including a number of very popular children's books.

The audience for *Conversations on Chemistry*

In her 'Preface', though she noted deficiencies in women's education, Mrs Marcet also felt 'encouraged by the establishment of those institutions, open to both sexes, for the dissemination of philosophical knowledge, which clearly proves that the general opinion no longer excludes women from an acquaintance with the elements of science'. Plate 20.3 certainly shows women (and some children) in attendance and taking notes, though not everyone viewed this favourably. Southey

Figure 20.9 21 Russell Square, London, at the turn of the twenty-first century. Photo: © Kim Sayer/CORBIS.

In 1808 the Marcets moved to 23 Russell Square, in the same terrace on the north side, two doors to the left of the house in this photograph. The terrace is now occupied by the University of London. The terracotta decorations were added in the 1890s. It was noted in the 1830s that Russell Square had 'from its first formation, been a favorite residence of the highest legal characters; and here merchants and bankers have seated themselves and families, the air and situation uniting to render it a pleasant retreat from the cares of business.' A commentator in the 1840s suggested that Russell Square was the home of the 'aristocracy of the City and the Inns of Court', and noted that the proximity of the British Museum and the London University (University College London) made it attractive to 'the scientific section of London literary men' (both quoted in Olsen, 1982, p.110).

suspected the women's motives: '[the] ladies were all upon the watch, and some score of them had their tablets and pencils, busily noting down what they heard, as topics for the next conversation party' (quoted in Foote, 1952, p.11). The Whig MP and co-founder of the *Edinburgh Review*, Francis Horner, who would later be a major promoter of education in the metropolis, had mixed feelings:

> I have once been to the Royal Institution and heard Davy lecture ... to a mixed and large assembly of both sexes, to the number of perhaps three hundred or more. It is a curious scene: the reflections it excites are of an ambiguous nature; for the prospect of possible good is mingled with the observation of much actual folly. The audience is assembled by the influence of fashion merely; and fashion and chemistry form a very incongruous union. At the same time it is a trophy to the sciences; one great advance is made towards the association of female and masculine minds in the pursuit of knowledge, and another domain of pleasing and liberal enquiry is included within the range of polished conversation.
>
> (Diary entry for 31 March 1802, quoted in Treneer, 1963, p.87)

Davy approved of the presence of women at his lectures as an indicator of social refinement and progress. However, their role was to be limited to understanding and transmitting culture. That is how Mrs Marcet, too, saw the matter. In 'Conversation I', the instructor Mrs B neatly delimits women's intellectual sphere:

> a woman may obtain such a knowledge of chemistry as will not only throw interest on the common occurrences of life, but will enlarge the sphere of her ideas, and render the contemplation of nature a source of delightful instruction.
>
> (Anthology II, p.161)

Conversations on Chemistry

Alexander Marcet was heavily involved in the preparation of *Conversations on Chemistry*. Her husband was the 'friend' to whom Jane Marcet turned for her conversations on chemistry and for assistance with repeating experiments. Bahar (2001) suggests that the 'friend' was in fact the whole of Alexander's scientific circle, including contacts in Geneva.

> First, Alexander chose the main ideas of an introductory course on chemistry that he delivered to her at home. Then they repeated together the principal experiments. Jane made a summary of the principles illustrated in each lecture on a set of small cards. She organized the cards into separate compartments in a small leather case and Alexander reviewed them, section by

> section. Each segment was then written out by Jane to become a dialogue in the *Conversations on Chemistry.*
>
> (Polkinghorn, 1993, pp.20–1)

The book is presented in dialogue form between a knowledgeable female instructor, Mrs B, and her two pupils, Emily and Caroline. Mrs B may have been named for Margaret Bryan, an earlier female author on science (Horrocks, 1987, p.61). Emily is the more serious of the two students. It has been suggested that the name is an anglicized and feminized reference to the character Émile, the hero of Rousseau's pedagogical work (Bahar, 2001, p.34). Caroline is slightly more frivolous, though both girls are sharp. Marcet suggests in the 'Preface' that she chose this form to emulate the kinds of conversations through which she herself had learned chemistry. It was 'familiar' and seemed an especially appropriate mode of instruction for females 'whose education is seldom calculated to prepare their minds for abstract ideas, or scientific language'. However, the form is part of a venerable tradition of didactic writing for men as well as women. At the same time, by giving her words to characters, Marcet also casts *Conversations on Chemistry* as a work of fiction. This device allows her to take on chemistry while remaining in the private, female territory of the home rather than claiming a public role (Myers, 1997, p.57). It also allows her to 'cheat' by cutting corners in her argument in a way that would not be possible in a public forum.

The sequence of lectures was similar to that of Humphry Davy's lecture syllabus of 1802, as her 'Preface' makes clear: 'treating first of the simplest bodies, and then gradually rising to the most intricate compounds'. Jane Marcet did not create a reference book for sampling information, but rather saw the work as an integrated whole which students should work through completely.

The strategy was a success. Quite apart from the sales figures, reviewers and readers alike agreed that the exposition was systematic and clear. An important component of the book is the elegant line drawings which illustrate experimental apparatus and procedures. The appearance of a hand in a drawing indicates that an experiment is to be performed. The absence of a hand indicates that the experiment is too complex or dangerous or expensive to be performed in the home.

EXERCISE Now read the extract from 'Conversation I' (Anthology II, pp.160–8) and then:

1 Note some similarities with the views in Davy's' 'Introductory Discourse'.

2 Note how many elements are listed by 1825.

3 Note the mechanism of chemical change.

4 Note where Mrs Marcet suggests that knowledge is tentative or provisional.

DISCUSSION

1 Chemistry is defined as the study of the intimate nature of substances and their mutual actions on each other. An understanding of chemistry is fundamental to understanding the other sciences since chemistry encompasses all things material. Chemistry is capable of numerous applications, such as in medicine and pharmacy. It also eases the human lot. Alchemy was misguided but nonetheless produced some enduring results.

2 After explaining that the ancient four-element theory has been superseded, Mrs Marcet says that as of 1825 there are 56 elementary substances, but she includes heat, light and electricity in the list, thereby adding tentatively a further weightless element.

3 Mrs Marcet puts forward Davy's view that chemical change occurs by means of chemical attraction, which is a power or force. She cites Davy on the possible electrical nature of chemical attraction.

4 For Mrs Marcet, a good deal of chemistry seems to be provisional. Chemistry progresses so certain views will inevitably change, moving 'nearer to the truth'. More elementary substances may be discovered. It is unclear whether chemical attraction is an inherent power of matter. Davy's view of electrical attraction is a hypothesis, which may or may not be right. While electricity is clearly implicated in chemical combinations, it is unclear whether electricity is a material agent (one of the 56 elements) or an inherent power of bodies.

Notice how Mrs Marcet has recourse to a divine explanation for chemical attraction. I chose to take your extracts from the tenth edition of 1825 because both Davy and Faraday helped to update it, and also because it was written long enough after the end of Davy's major scientific work for that to be included. That is, the 1806 edition included neither of the Bakerian lectures nor the material on chlorine. However, the effort of keeping up to date is telling on the 1825 edition. Few would have claimed by then that heat, light and electricity should be on the list of elementary substances. Davy's influence could also be a drawback – there is no mention of the work of John Dalton and his atomic hypothesis alongside the discussion of elementary substances: 'Simplicity has charms, only so far as it accords with truth.'

7 Sir Humphry Davy in the metropolis: the final years

In the spring of 1812 Davy was knighted by the Prince Regent, married a wealthy widow and resigned his chair at the Royal Institution, though he intended to continue to do research there. The marriage proved to be an unhappy one, but Davy was occupied with lecture tours, preparing his *Agricultural Chemistry* for publication, and writing a far from successful textbook, *Elements of Chemical Philosophy*. He also became involved in various practical projects with mixed success. In 1813 he made the first of several continental trips, including a visit to France authorized specifically by Napoleon, so that he could collect the electrical prize awarded to him some six years before and to meet with French scientists. While travelling in Italy on another occasion, he researched ancient pigments with a view to reproducing them chemically. However, Davy never got back to systematic scientific research. Knight suggests that, having given up lecturing, Davy lost the stimulus of synergy between his lecturing and his research activities (1992, pp.95–6).

President of the Royal Society

In 1821 Davy sat for a portrait by Sir Thomas Lawrence, one of the most prominent European portrait painters of his generation. This is Sir Humphry Davy, Baronet, with his famous scientific work behind him, but at the height of his social prestige in the first year of his presidency of the Royal Society.

EXERCISE Compare the portrayal of Davy in the copy of the 1821 Lawrence portrait (Figure 20.10) with that in the 1803 Howard portrait (Plate 20.4).

DISCUSSION In the 1821 portrait Davy is dressed much more flashily and ready for the outdoors, as if interrupted on his way out, a man of action. Indeed the outdoors – nature – can be glimpsed over his shoulder, where the sun is setting on a mature Davy. He is standing rather than seated, and his expression is determined, indeed arrogant, and somewhat restless rather than contemplative.

On a table on which Davy leans his right hand is a symbol not of laboratory science but of science applied for the benefit of humanity (and industry), a safety lamp. The pose is characteristic of Lawrence's aristocratic portraits. Davy and Lawrence were friends. Like Davy, Lawrence had deployed his talents to achieve an upward social path

Figure 20.10 Anonymous (after Sir Thomas Lawrence), Sir Humphry Davy, Bt, *c.1821, oil on canvas, 142.2 x 111.8 cm, National Portrait Gallery, London.*

from humble beginnings. He was knighted in 1815 and became president of the Royal Academy in 1820, the same year that Davy took up the presidency of the Royal Society. These two premier national bodies for art and science were both located in Somerset House. Lawrence understood what Davy had achieved (Knight, 2001, p.41). Lawrence was elected to the Fellowship of the Royal Society early in 1822. Davy headed the list of proposers of this 'gentleman not less distinguished for his service in art, than for his ardent desire to promote useful knowledge' (Royal Society archives, ref: GB117 The Royal Society EC/1821/40). Shortly after Davy's death in 1829, Lady Davy offered Lawrence's portrait to the Royal Society as a memorial to her recently deceased husband. It still hangs there. This was in keeping with Davy's wishes. When near death, he had had his eye on posterity and had asked her to make 'all arrangements which may make my memory useful to the world, and awaken kind feelings of my friends' (quoted in Prescott, 2001, p.135).

It is safe to assume that Davy chose to be represented with the miners' safety lamp. This is a symbol not of the search for knowledge, but rather of knowledge utilized, of science at its most public. It is a symbol in keeping with the Enlightenment scientific agenda of Sir Joseph Banks, which you may recall from Units 12–13. Born in the first of Banks's 41 years as president of the Royal Society, Davy was his successor in that role. Banks had approved of the safety lamp:

> My dear Sir Humphry
>
> Many thanks for your kind letter, which has given me unspeakable pleasure. Much as, by the more brilliant discoveries you have made, the Royal Society has been exalted in the opinion of the scientific world, I am of the opinion that the solid and effective reputation of that body will be more advanced among our cotemporaries [*sic*] of all ranks by your present discovery, than it has been by all the rest. To have come forward when called upon, because no one else could discover means of defending society from a tremendous scourge of humanity, and to have, by the application of enlightened philosophy, found the means of providing a certain precautionary measure effectual to guard mankind for the future against all this alarming and increasing evil, cannot fail to recommend the discoverer to much public gratitude, and to place the Royal Society in a more popular point of view than all the abstruse discoveries beyond the understanding of unlearned people ...
>
> (Joseph Banks to Humphry Davy, November 1815, quoted in Knight, 1992, pp.109–10)

Indeed, honours followed; it was for this work that Davy was made a baronet in 1818. In addition to being an example of science applied for economic benefit, the lamp was an example of science used for humanitarian ends: to save the lives of miners. It was well known that

Davy did not patent the device, thus altruistically 'giving' his science to the nation. Associating himself with the lamp in this public manner in the Lawrence portrait was also a way of stating that it was a 'Davy' lamp – that is, of defending his claim to be its inventor. This had been challenged by the supporters of George Stephenson, a provincial engineer who had arrived at a similar device by trial and error methods. In the end, it was the high-profile targeted application of science in the setting of a metropolitan research laboratory that won plaudits from the scientific establishment.

EXERCISE Now examine how the safety lamp works in 'A dictionary of chemistry' on the CD-ROM or in the Activities Booklet (ALE 10).

Davy's presidency of the Royal Society, which lasted until early 1827, is generally regarded as having been neither a successful nor a happy period. Banks's long presidency had cast the Royal Society in an Enlightenment mould of gentlemanly patronage of science, especially natural history, which he linked to imperial and commercial concerns (recall Units 12–13). Evidence of scientific activity was not a requirement for membership, though appropriate social and political connections seem to have been. From early in the century, a number of new, specialist societies with their own scientific agendas and a different social base, such as that exemplified by the Marcet circle, began to take shape outside Banks's purview. Members of such bodies came to constitute a reforming party within the Royal Society even before Davy's presidency. Though keenly aware of his own acquired social status and its relevance to his gaining the presidency as someone who had made his way by science, Davy had some sympathy for the reform movement. Among other measures, he took steps to normalize relations with the specialist societies, worked towards establishing scientific criteria for membership, and sought to widen the base of government support for science beyond Banksian imperial goals. He was active in establishing the Athenaeum club as an alternative location for informal intellectual discussion or, to use a modern term, networking. Furthermore, he was instrumental with Stanford Raffles in founding the London zoo.

However, Davy was caught 'between hostile camps', as Miller (1983, p.1) puts it. The pace of reform was both too fast for the traditional interests and too slow for the reformers, who were disillusioned by the mid-1820s. This would not have surprised Banks, who had not wanted Davy to be his successor, thinking him 'rather too lively to fill the chair of the Royal Society with that degree of gravity which it is most becoming to assume' (Treneer, 1963, p.183). Knight concludes that Davy had over-reached himself:

> What was expected of the new President was such that nobody could have met it; Davy's popularity fell and his anger became notorious as he tried to be domineering ...
>
> To have a man, however able, whose schooling had been sketchy and whose upbringing had been plebian and provincial running such a society is amazing; what is not amazing is that this experiment of Davy's did not work. He could not play the autocrat as Banks, a great landed proprietor, had done, and his social unease seemed haughtiness. His research had been solitary, and while his science was admired and he had achieved recognition, he was not loved. The important thing with social mobility, as Faraday [Davy's famous successor at the RI who had similarly humble origins] learned partly from watching Davy, is to know where to stop.
>
> (Knight, 1992, p.7)

Towards the end of 1826, Davy suffered the first of what would be a series of strokes and went into retirement; he resigned the presidency in 1827. His final two years were marred by ill health but productive of two small books in dialogue form: *Salmonia*, which was about fishing and his great love of the outdoors, and *Consolations in Travel*, an exegesis of his chemical philosophy. In it he rejected materialism, and reiterated his Romantic view of nature and his belief that nature displayed the wisdom and beneficence of God.

A figure whose life and work straddled the Enlightenment and the Romantic, Davy was in many ways a transitional figure between natural philosopher and scientist. He was transitional, too, because he performed in an institutional laboratory context, albeit one that retained the atmosphere of a gentlemen's club. He was a brilliant experimenter whose chemical work was well recognized in his own time. However, his reluctance to theorize, his withdrawal from active research so early, and the fact that chemistry moved rapidly in other directions meant that 'Davy did not leave the gap one might have expected in the scientific community' (Knight, 1992, p.169). Near the end of his life, Davy wrote a brief rhapsody to nature which provides his own evaluation of his achievements:

> Oh, most magnificent and noble Nature!
> Have I not worshipped thee with such a love
> As never mortal man before displayed?
> Adored thee in thy majesty of visible creation,
> And searched into thy hidden and mysterious ways
> As Poet, as Philosopher, as Sage?
>
> (Davy, 1858, p.14)

References

Bahar, S. (2001) 'Jane Marcet and the limits to public science', *British Journal for the History of Science*, vol.34, pp.29–49.

Berman, M. (1978) *Social Change and Scientific Organization: The Royal Institution, 1799–1844*, London, Heinemann Educational.

Brock, W.H. (1992) *The Fontana History of Chemistry*, London, Fontana Press.

Carter, H.B. (ed.) (1979) *The Sheep and Wool Correspondence of Sir Joseph Banks, 1781–1820*, Norwich, Library Council of NSW and British Museum (Natural History).

Chilton, D. and Coley, N.G. (1980) 'The laboratories of the Royal Institution in the 19th century', *Ambix*, vol.27, pp.173–203.

Crosland, M. (1967) *The Society of Arcueil: A View of French Science at the Time of Napoleon I*, London, Heinemann.

Crosland, M. (1987) 'The image of science as a threat: Burke versus Priestley and the "Philosophic Revolution"', *British Journal for the History of Science*, vol.20, pp.277–307.

Davy, J. (ed.) (1839a) *Collected Works of Sir Humphry Davy, Bart., Volume II: Early Miscellaneous Papers*, London, Smith, Elder and Co. (reprinted 2001 by Thoemmes Press).

Davy, J. (ed.) (1839b) *Collected Works of Sir Humphry Davy, Bart., Volume III: Researches Chiefly Concerning Nitrous Oxide*, London, Smith, Elder and Co. (reprinted 2001 by Thoemmes Press).

Davy, J. (ed.) (1840) *Collected Works of Sir Humphry Davy, Bart., Volume VII: Discourses Delivered before the Royal Society and Agricultural Lectures, Part I,* London, Smith, Elder and Co. (reprinted 2001 by Thoemmes Press).

Davy, J. (ed.) (1858) *Fragmentary Remains, Literary and Scientific, of Sir Humphry Davy, Bart.*, London, John Churchill.

Egerton, J. (ed.) (1990) *Wright of Derby*, exhibition catalogue, London, Tate Gallery.

Elliott, P. (2000) 'The birth of public science in the English provinces: natural philosophy in Derby, c.1690–1760', *Annals of Science*, vol.57, pp.61–100.

Foote, G.A. (1952) 'Sir Humphry Davy and his audience at the Royal Institution', *ISIS*, vol.43, pp.6–12.

Fraser, D. (1990) 'Joseph Wright of Derby and the Lunar Society', in J. Egerton (ed.) *Wright of Derby*, London, Tate Gallery, pp.15–24.

Fullmer, J.Z. (1960) 'Letter to the Editor', *Scientific American*, vol.203, no.2, August, pp.12–14.

Fullmer, J.Z. (2000) *Young Humphry Davy: The Making of an Experimental Chemist*, Philadelphia, American Philosophical Society.

Gascoigne, J. (1998) *Science in the Service of Empire: Joseph Banks, the British State and the Uses of Science in the Age of Revolution*, Cambridge, Cambridge University Press.

Gauja, P. and Delom, M.T. (1966) *Académie des Sciences, troisème centenaire, 1666–1966: quelques souvenirs*, Paris, Institute de France.

Golinski, J. (1992) *Science as Public Culture: Chemistry and Enlightenment in Britain, 1760–1820*, Cambridge, Cambridge University Press.

Horrocks, S. (1987) 'Audiences for chemistry in Regency Britain: Mrs Marcet's *Conversations on Chemistry*', undergraduate dissertation, Corpus Christi College, University of Cambridge.

James, F.A.J.L. (2000) *Guides to the Royal Institution of Great Britain: 1 – History*, London, Royal Institution of Great Britain.

Knight, D.M. (1992) *Humphry Davy: Science and Power*, Cambridge, Cambridge University Press.

Knight, D.M. (2001) 'Davy's visions', in J. Hamilton (ed.) *Fields of Influence: Conjunctions of Artists and Scientists, 1815–1860*, Birmingham, University of Birmingham Press, pp.31–49.

Lawrence, C. (1990) 'The power and the glory: Humphry Davy and Romanticism', in A. Cunningham and N. Jardine (eds) *Romanticism and the Sciences*, Cambridge, Cambridge University Press, pp.213–27.

Levere, T.H. (1981) *Poetry Realized in Nature: Samuel Taylor Coleridge and Early Nineteenth-Century Science*, Cambridge, Cambridge University Press.

Matthiesen Gallery (2001, online) 'European paintings: Alexandre Evariste Fragonard', http://www.europeanpaintings.com/exhibits/romantic/fragbio.htm [accessed 18 April 2002].

Miller, D.P. (1983) 'Between hostile camps: Sir Humphry Davy's presidency of the Royal Society of London, 1820–1827', *British Journal for the History of Science*, vol.16, pp.1–47.

Morton, A.Q. and Wess, J. (1993) *Public and Private Science: The King George III Collection*, London, Oxford University Press in association with the Science Museum.

Myers, G. (1997) 'Fictionality, demonstration, and a forum for popular science: Jane Marcet's *Conversations on Chemistry*', in B.T. Gates and A.B. Shteir (eds) *Natural Eloquence: Women Reinscribe Science*, Madison, University of Wisconsin Press, pp.43–60.

Olsen, D.J. (1982) *Town Planning in London: The Eighteenth and Nineteenth Centuries*, 2nd edn, New Haven and London, Yale University Press.

Paris, J.A. (1831) *The Life of Sir Humphry Davy, Bart.*, 2 vols, London, Colburn and Bentley.

Polkinghorn, B. (1993) *Jane Marcet: An Uncommon Woman*, Aldermaston, Forestwood.

Porter, R. (1980) 'The Enlightenment in England', in R. Porter and M. Teich (eds) *The Enlightenment in National Context*, Cambridge, Cambridge University Press, pp.1–18.

Porter, R. (1992) *Doctor of Society: Thomas Beddoes and the Sick Trade in Late Enlightenment England*, London, Routledge.

Prescott, G. (2001) 'Gleams of glory: forging learned society portrait collections', in J. Hamilton (ed.) *Fields of Influence: Conjunctions of Artists and Scientists, 1815–1860*, Birmingham, University of Birmingham Press, pp.129–62.

Schupbach, W. (1987) 'A select iconography of animal experiment', in N.A. Rupke (ed.) *Vivisection in Historical Perspective*, London, Croom Helm, pp.340–61.

Shapin, S. and Schaffer, S. (1985) *Leviathan and the Air Pump: Hobbes, Boyle, and the Experimental Life*, Princeton, Princeton University Press.

Sharrock, R. (1962) 'The chemist and the poet: Sir Humphry Davy and the preface to *Lyrical Ballads*', *Notes and Records of the Royal Society*, vol.17, pp.57–76.

Solkin, D. (1992) 'ReWrighting Shaftesbury: the *Air Pump* and the limits of commercial humanism', in J. Barrell (ed.) *Painting and the Politics of Culture: New Essays on British Art, 1700–1850*, Oxford, Oxford University Press, pp.73–99.

Stewart, L. (1992) *The Rise of Public Science: Rhetoric, Technology, and Natural Philosophy in Newtonian Britain*, Cambridge, Cambridge University Press.

Treneer, A. (1963) *The Mercurial Chemist: A Life of Sir Humphry Davy*, London, Methuen & Co Ltd.

Uglow, Jenny (2002) *The Lunar Men: The Friends Who Made the Future, 1730–1810,* London, Faber.

WGBH Interactive (1998, online) 'Africans in America, Part 2, Resource Book', http://www.pbs.org/wgbh/aia/part2/2h67.html [accessed 10 September 2003].

Further reading

Brock, W.H. (1992) *The Fontana History of Chemistry*, London, Fontana Press, chapters 3 and 4.

Golinski, J. (1992) *Science as Public Culture: Chemistry and Enlightenment in Britain, 1760–1820*, Cambridge, Cambridge University Press (pb 1999).

Knight, D.M. (1992) *Humphry Davy: Science and Power*, Cambridge, Cambridge University Press.

Uglow, Jenny (2002) *The Lunar Men: The Friends Who Made the Future, 1730–1810*, London, Faber.

Units 22–23
Sir John Soane: Enlightenment Romantic

Prepared for the course team by Tim Benton

Contents

Study components

Weeks of study	*Supplementary material*	*Audio-visual*	*Anthologies and set books*	*CD-ROM*
2	Activities Booklet Illustrations Book	Video 3	Anthology II	*Sir John Soane's Museum*

These units focus on the astonishing house and museum which the English architect Sir John Soane left to the nation by Act of Parliament in 1833, along with his library, papers and possessions. This building and its contents are therefore the 'text' that forms the core of the two weeks' work. To better explore this 'text', we are providing an introductory video and a CD-ROM that includes a 'virtual reality' version of the house and contents. Objects and rooms in the CD-ROM are indicated with this icon: ◎. If you are unable to use the CD-ROM, the video includes an introduction and a tour of the house which will allow you to get a good idea of its contents, sufficient to follow most of the exercises in the Activities Booklet. Nevertheless, without the CD-ROM, you will not be able to look up all the objects referred to, so the units allow you to focus on other aspects of Soane's life and work. The units are divided into a biographical section, an introduction to Soane's ideas and architectural style, and a history of his house and museum. If you choose to focus on the house and its contents using the CD-ROM, you may spend less time on the life. These units contain a lot of information on people, objects and architectural features; be selective in making detailed notes, bearing in mind the TMA and your own interests.

Aims

- To interrogate Sir John Soane's life and career to gain an understanding of the issues of the day, the passions, curiosities and pressures influencing a well-read and innovative architect.
- To explore the construction of Sir John Soane's house and the formation of his collection as a commentary on architectural style, as testimony to Soane's practice as an architect, as evidence of his personal life, as an insight into Soane's mind, and as an evolving model of memory, instruction, philanthropy, curiosity and collection.
- To assess the extent to which Soane moved from an Enlightenment to a Romantic sensibility during his lifetime.

Objectives

By the end of your work on Units 22–23 you should be able:

- to evaluate Soane's biography in order to form an opinion of his character and motivation;
- to recognize the features of different kinds of classical architecture and understand some of the issues involved in their use and criticism;
- to interpret writings by Soane and others as examples of classical, picturesque and Romantic attitudes.

1 Introduction

When Sir John Soane died on 20 January 1837, he had come a long way from his origins in Goring-on-Thames. Born John Soan (without the final 'e'), the youngest son of a bricklayer, on 10 September 1753, he had clawed his way into the architectural profession by hard work and application, had been received by the highest levels of society, and had been awarded the highest honours available to an architect of his day. And yet he was a frustrated, often irascible and bitter man whose highest ambitions in public architecture had been denied and who felt himself marginalized and misunderstood. Despite the admiration produced in many of his contemporaries by his architecture and ideas, Soane did not found a school of architecture, nor did he significantly alter the development of architectural style during his lifetime.

To understand Soane the architect, however, we must try to understand his character. His sensitivity and sometimes pathological irrationality and spitefulness to those, including family members, who had wronged him have to be balanced against the fact that he had many loyal friends who stood by him in difficult times. In particular, the people he dealt with in his working relations, both clients and workmen, admired and respected his professionalism, precision, honesty and loyalty. In this he was unusual, at a time when many architects lacked either the competence or the will to overcome the many frustrations of building work in town or country. He was the most efficient, economical and conscientious architect of his generation, and one of the most sophisticated technically. Throughout his career, but especially in the first ten years of his professional practice (1780–90), Soane was prepared to travel almost constantly all over Britain, to supervise jobs in hand, even when these consisted of relatively modest additions or modifications to existing buildings. But apart from this bedrock of sound professional practice and solid relationships, almost everything about Soane's personal and professional life appears contradictory.

Highly innovative in stylistic terms, Soane was also a fanatical classicist who criticized all about him, including his own works, for breaking the rules of classical architecture. And these rules he pursued into a labyrinth of antique and recent theory and practice. He was the best read of his architectural contemporaries, although never able fully to assimilate and synthesize his learning. He wanted to pin down reasons and meanings for every aspect of architectural decoration, but at the same time he believed passionately in the poetry of architecture, in the manipulation of 'mysterious light', in individual invention. Soane was a man of the Enlightenment in that he believed passionately in the acquisition of knowledge and the perfectibility of people and things by the application of reason. On the other hand, his architectural reputation rests essentially on what he called the search for 'character' in building: in other words, his individuality, a Romantic quality. Romantic, too, were his obsession with death, his fascination with the picturesque and the sublime, his paranoia and self-image as a persecuted genius. Driven by strong and often uncontrolled emotions of affection or antipathy, he seems to have found it acceptable, and even necessary, to present a series of strong contradictions to the outside world. These contradictions make his writings and his relationships difficult to understand, but they enriched his architecture. And in arguably his greatest (and certainly the best preserved) achievement – his own house and museum – the mental contradictions and their paradoxical productions take centre ground.

EXERCISE I want you now to view the short introduction to the house (Video 3, band 3). This is a taster, intended to give you some idea of what we will be dealing with. It is meant to be a bit mysterious. Later, you will explore the house and its contents in more detail. Do Exercise 1 in the Activities Booklet now.

EXERCISE With this brief and partial tour of the house, it would be a good idea now to familiarize yourself with the floor plans of the house. Work through the section on 'Reading architectural plans' in the Activities Booklet and then spend some time studying Plates 22.1–22.3 in the Illustrations Book.

Note: in the units I frequently refer to objects or rooms in Sir John Soane's Museum on the CD-ROM. I have used the icon ◎ to indicate this. If you have access to a computer, you can look these up on the CD-ROM, but it is not essential and I would advise you *not* to do so on a first read through. Instructions on how to find rooms are given on the CD-ROM. Objects referred to more specifically will have a CD-ROM number (e.g. CD-ROM 23); these images can be found, all together, on the CD-ROM. I suggest you spend a little time now familiarizing yourself with how the CD-ROM works. The Activities Booklet tells you how to install it; once you have done that, work through 'How to use this CD-ROM' on screen. Explore the house on the CD-ROM and on Video 3, band 4, activity 1. Please note that the course's assessment strategy will also accommodate those without the use of a computer, and students not using the CD-ROM can ignore the icon ◎ references.

2 Life

Soane's father, John Soan (1714–68), was a bricklayer from Goring-on-Thames, near Reading in the Thames Valley. Soane was born in 1753, the last of a family of six, of whom two died in infancy. His brother William (born in 1741) remained a bricklayer all his life. Soane seems to have been educated in Reading at a private school run by a William Baker, whose fondness for collecting books made a big impression on the young boy. When John Soan Sr died in 1768, the family moved to Chertsea (now Chertsey) in Surrey, where William Soan had gone to live. Soane and his wife would spend many days and weeks in and around Chertsea, whose attractions included, for Soane, excellent fishing. Young John helped out on his brother's building sites, where he may have picked up some of his later expertise in masonry construction. When Soane came to write his memoirs two years before his death, he eliminated all trace of his family and childhood.

In 1768 the 15-year-old boy was introduced to James Peacock, a surveyor who worked closely with the successful London architect George Dance Jr, and Peacock in turn secured him a job of some sort in Dance's office. So, in 1768, Soane went to live in Dance's house on Chiswell Street in the City of London. Dance had returned in 1764 from six years in Italy at his architect father's expense, where he had made measured drawings of the Temple of Vesta at Tivoli and achieved membership of the Academies of Parma and San Luca in Rome. Dance was a founder member of the Royal Academy in 1769, one of only five architects, and had a good architectural library, which stimulated the young Soane to learn about architectural theory. But later, in 1805, when Dance was made Professor of Architecture at the Royal Academy, Soane successfully plotted to take his place. Soane's life story was an uncomfortable mixture of loyalty, friendship, betrayal and accusations.

Apprenticeship

Soane was in Dance's office while Newgate Prison, Dance's most exciting new project in London, was designed and built (◎CD-ROM 01). An example of Dance's intelligent classicism was his remodelling of All Hallows Church, London (see Plate 22.4). Soane also played a role in Dance's renovation of Pitzhanger Manor, the Ealing house of Thomas Gurnell in 1769. Thirty-one years later, Soane would be able to buy this house from the Gurnell estate and carry out his own renovation. Well-read, amusing, talented as a draughtsman and musician, Dance encouraged Soane to improve himself in all aspects of the business, and in October 1771 Soane was accepted as a student at the Royal Academy Schools.

The Professor of Architecture at the Royal Academy, Thomas Sandby (1721–98), gave the lectures which the architecture students had to attend, and Soane would copy much of the content in his own lectures after 1806. In 1813 Soane also followed Sandby as architect to the Freemasons (whose Hall Sandby had designed in 1771). In 1772 Soane was sent by Dance to work for Henry Holland (1745–1806), another influential figure whose work bore the brunt of Soane's scorn later in life. Soane worked as a clerk for Holland on a respectable salary of £60 per year, and was introduced to the details of professional management of a range of building sites, from country houses to urban development. Much of Soane's future reputation for efficiency was acquired in Holland's office, which was one of the most successful practices of the day. Later, Soane invariably referred to Holland as a 'bricklayer', and he saw him as an architect fatally compromised by his entrepreneurial activities (Holland made a fortune developing the wealthy London suburb of Hans Town, now part of Chelsea, and his work for the Prince Regent at the Brighton Pavilion is discussed in Unit 31). And yet Soane retained a close personal friendship with Henry Holland's son Richard, who was also a builder and entrepreneur, and employed his firm on a number of occasions. After Henry Holland died in 1806, Soane purchased the cream of his collection of antique fragments, collected by Charles Heathcote Tatham in Rome, which the Trustees of the British Museum had declined to accept (this collection is displayed in the ◎Study).

In 1772 Soane won the Royal Academy silver medal with his elevation drawing of Inigo Jones's Banqueting House in Whitehall (1619–22) (◎Breakfast Parlour at No. 12). Later he would have the job of refacing the venerable building in Portland stone. Inigo Jones had introduced the style of Italian **Renaissance** architect Andrea Palladio to England, and this was later taken up by the Earl of Burlington and his followers in the early eighteenth century as the basis for the style known as **neo-Palladianism**. In 1776, at the second attempt, Soane won the coveted Royal Academy gold medal for his design of a triumphal bridge crossing the Thames near Lambeth Bridge (see Plate 22.5 – different versions of this are in ◎Picture Room and North Drawing Room). A favourite topic for idealized, unrealistic designs, this project allowed Soane to display his close attention to the use of the **orders**[5] and skill in the manipulation of spaces.

Italian tour

With the proceeds of his gold medal travel grant, Soane set off on 17 March 1778 for a voyage to Italy. The two years he spent there not only rounded out and completed his architectural education, but also supplied him with a network of clients who would keep him professionally active for the next few years and launch his career. En route to Italy, Soane visited Paris, where he saw the newest works by French neoclassical architects, including Soufflot's Ste Geneviève, still under construction (see Plate 22.6). This church was given a new role under the French Revolution as the Panthéon, not to be confused with the antique building known as the Pantheon in Rome (◎CD-ROM 03).

[5] A term used to describe the ways in which columns, entablatures and pedestals were combined in classical architecture (see glossary).

In Rome by 2 May, Soane began an intense programme of measuring and drawing the ruins and making contacts among the British community. One such who was a generous host and lively travelling companion in Italy, but whose offers of work on his estates in Ireland later proved illusory, was Frederick Hervey, Bishop of Derry. A characteristic product of their witty exchanges was the design for a 'Canine Residence' – a neoclassical dog kennel – which Soane drew to amuse the bishop's friends in 1778 (◎Dressing Room, CD-ROM 04). He did introduce Soane to a number of very worthwhile future patrons, including the talented amateur architect Thomas Pitt (later Lord Camelford), whose younger cousin William Pitt the Younger (for many years prime minister) would also later become a loyal client. Wealthy and ambitious young men like these provided Soane with the commissions on which his career was founded between his return to Britain in 1780 and his winning of the key job to the Bank of England in 1788. Many of them remained his friends for the rest of his life. While in Italy Soane took care to keep his image alive at the Royal Academy, sending home beautifully rendered perspectives of a so-called 'Design for a British Senate House', an idealized building combining all the functions of the House of Commons and House of Lords (see Plate 22.7 and ◎CD-ROM 05, North Drawing Room). This grandiose scheme, stimulated by the sight of the ruins of the Roman baths, laid the seeds of a lifetime obsession to create a new House of Lords at Whitehall.

Soane also met a number of collectors, including Stefano Borgia at Velletri. He developed a taste for the heterogeneous collections of antiquities of all kinds formed from the Renaissance period onwards and often presented in imaginative and evocative ways. The collection which most influenced him was that at the Villa Albani in Rome. Soane was impressed both by the high quality of the objects, in part selected by Johann Winckelmann, and by the manner of their display, in niches and with mirror glass used to extend the illusion of space behind them. Soane owned three French editions of Winckelmann's *Geschichte der Kunst des Althertums* (*The History of the Art of Antiquity*, first published 1764, French edition 1781) and was much influenced by Winckelmann's passionate approval of classical Greek art. In the grounds of the villa stood a folly: an aviary designed in the form of a ruined temple by Carlo Marchionni. The pleasure of artificial ruins, and the amusement of imagining how the folly might have looked before its partial collapse, remained with Soane, and he designed follies of his own in his houses at Pitzhanger and Lincoln's Inn Fields (◎CD-ROM 36–39).

Most importantly, Soane visited the archaeological sites in Rome and in and around Naples, including Pompeii, Paestum and Herculaneum. He met Giovanni Battista Piranesi (1720–78) a few months before his death, on the recommendation of Sir William Chambers, founder member and treasurer of the Royal Academy. Piranesi created a reputation as a passionate advocate of Roman, as opposed to Greek, classical architecture. In his book *Parere sull'architettura* (*An Approach to*

Architecture, 1765), Pireanesi advocated using Roman examples in inventive ways to create a new style. The old man gave him four engravings, and Soane avidly collected watercolours and engravings by Piranesi and his son (◎Breakfast Parlour at No. 12, Picture Room, CD-ROM 06). The importance of Piranesi for Soane was that his representations of Roman and Greek ruins were far more than archaeological reconstructions. They combined a Romantic sensibility for the pathos of ruins with a sublime sense of the grandeur and vast scale of ancient buildings. Soane encouraged his more able draughtsmen to emulate the Romantic sensibility of Piranesi's watercolours and engravings. He later bought the sumptuous volumes of William Hamilton's *Campi Phlegraei* (1776–99), a study of volcanic activity around Vesuvius and Mount Etna, including archaeological sites excavated in the area (◎CD-ROM 08). The excitement of discovering half-buried fragments of past glories comes over well in the illustrations by Pietro Fabris. During a long trip to Sicily, he visited the bizarre Villa Palagonia in Bagheria, whose interiors were lined in mirrors made from sheets of mica[6] (see Plate 22.8). In his enthusiastic response to this very unorthodox **Baroque** building, Soane revealed the eclecticism of his taste and his refusal to be pigeon-holed as a pure classicist, even if he later thundered against the excesses of this and other Baroque buildings during his Royal Academy lectures.

Soane also made friends among the artists and hangers-on in the English community who remained loyal to him all his life. One such was the talented painter Maria Hadfield, who married the painter Richard Cosway in 1781 and who opened a fashionable salon at their home in Schomberg House in Pall Mall. Soane later bought a number of items from the Cosway sale (*Bull breaking the Egg*, ◎Dressing Room; and *Charles II* by Arnold Quellin, ◎Monk's Parlour). A fascinating woman, Maria had intense friendships and affairs with a number of famous people, including the French neoclassical painter Jacques-Louis David and the highly eccentric antiquarian Baron d'Hancarville (actually Pierre-François Hugues). Soane became fascinated with Baron d'Hancarville's bizarre theories, later buying his book *Recherches sur l'origine, l'esprit et les progrès des arts de la Grèce* … (*Investigations into the Origin, Spirit and Progress of the Arts in Greece*, 1785) and heavily annotating it. D'Hancarville believed that all forms of religion and creativity in the visual arts were related to primitive beliefs expressed in Priapic rituals and sexual symbolism. For d'Hancarville, the Hindu Siva, the Greek Dionysus and the Roman Bacchus were personifications of the same fundamental belief. It was from d'Hancarville that Soane acquired an interest in the motif of the bull breaking the egg – according to d'Hancarville one of the first images of the creation of the world.

Another creative artist in Rome, and a friend of Maria Hadfield, was the sculptor Thomas Banks, whom Soane would employ on a number of

[6] A mineral that is split into sheets to make a reflective surface.

occasions and whose works he collected (◎Flaxman Recess and Anteroom). Banks was a loyal ally during the in-fighting at the Royal Academy and was commissioned by Soane on various occasions to produce architectural reliefs in imitation of the antique (◎Anteroom and Museum). Banks carved the marble chimney pieces representing Indian women returning from the Ganges in Daylesford House, designed by the architect S.P. Cockerell. This was the house built (1788–93) for Warren Hastings, who had been Governor-General of India and was a passionate advocate of the quality and antiquity of Indian culture. Banks gave Soane a strange sculpture, *The Hindu Deity Krishna, or Camadeva with One of his Wives on a Crocodile* (◎Anteroom). This sculpture, typical of the Indian-influenced work Banks carried out for Cockerell, meshed with Soane's interest in d'Hancarville's ideas. Soane's fascination with all kinds of exotic information marks him as typical of the restless mentality of turn-of-the century intellectuals.

Soane's Italian trip furnished him with friends, patrons, drawings and memories which would fuel his architecture throughout his life. In the unbuttoned world of the Grand Tour, far from the controlling influence of family and society, young men of the aristocracy and the newly wealthy could mix freely with the talented and the ambitious who took the trouble to learn a little Italian, study their guidebooks and supply a little culture. Later in life he recalled the trip in glowing terms and dreamed of returning. In some ways, many of the objects in Lincoln's Inn Fields, as well as documenting the architecture of antiquity in Italy, recalled for Soane his happy years travelling and discovering.

Building the career

Soon after his return from Italy in 1780, Soane's career began to build on the basis of contacts from friends made in Italy, and by 1783 he was designing his first new country house, Letton Hall in Norfolk. Soane quickly had as much work as he could handle restoring, extending and replanning country houses all over Britain. (See ◎CD-ROM 09, his design for a rustic dairy for his friend the Hon. Philip Yorke at his house in Hamels, Hertfordshire; CD-ROM 10, his design for stables at Betchworth Castle, 1799, for Henry Peters; and CD-ROM 11, a sketch for Saxlingham Rectory, Norfolk, for Revd John Gooch, 1784–6.) It is important to realize that Soane managed to preserve excellent relations with most of these clients, whatever the difficulties of meeting their needs and overcoming the many obstacles of building work and accountability. As one satisfied client brought him another, Soane could soon count among his clients and friends many of the top names in the City and Whitehall. For example, Samuel Bosanquet, cousin of one of his travelling companions, was a director of the Bank of England and the Levant Company, and Bosanquet's cousin Jacob was a director of the East India Company.

Soane was also a loyal and trusted friend of many of the builders and craftsmen he employed on his jobs. For example, he frequently employed Edward Foxhall (a fellow student at the Royal Academy) as decorator and Richard Holland (son of his second master Henry Holland) as builder. It was in this professional world that Soane met his future wife Eliza Smith, ward of the successful builder George Wyatt. Wyatt held important posts in the City, as the City builder and the Surveyor of Paving in the City. He was also a considerable property owner. Although an obituary in the *Gentleman's Magazine* claimed that George was the brother of the very successful architect James Wyatt (1746–1813), this has not been confirmed. Eliza kept house for George for several years after the death of her parents, and knew the variegated professional world of builders and architects, patrons and tradesmen well.

On 21 August 1784, John Soane (having added the 'e' to his name) married Eliza Smith, who was to be his professional ally as well as loyal companion (◎South Drawing Room, Flaxman portrait). Two sons died in infancy and the elder of the others, John, was a sickly child. The younger, George, became a great worry to his parents, as we shall see (◎South Drawing Room, double portrait of George and John Soane). Soane had hoped that, like the great eighteenth-century architectural dynasties (for example, the Dance and Wyatt families), his sons might be persuaded to take on the family name as architects. John Jr did have talent as a draughtsman and raised Soane's hopes (◎CD-ROM 12). But he lacked ambition and will, and his continuing ill-health ruled out a career as an architect. George was always a rebel and soon distanced himself as far as possible from architecture, taking up a precarious existence as a poet and playwright. Twice gaoled for debt and irresponsible in his personal relationships, George finally took the unpardonable step of publishing two anonymous attacks on his father's architecture in *The Champion* in September 1815. Soane was convinced that these 'death blows' hastened the untimely death of Eliza Soane in November of the same year, and he framed and exhibited the fatal evidence, first in the South Drawing Room and then in his bedroom.

When George Wyatt died in 1790, Soane was left property and shares which allowed him a comfortable income for the rest of his life. A fitting end to this first phase of his professional career was the publication of a volume of his domestic work, *Plans ... of Buildings Erected in the Counties of Norfolk, Suffolk etc.*, early in 1789. In addition to publicizing his work, this book also enabled Soane to spell out his professional code of conduct. The significance of the volume lay partly in its dedication (to the king) and the list of influential subscribers, who included William Pitt (the prime minister), Lord Chancellor Hardwicke and a number of other well-placed clients, as well as fellow architects like Sir William Chambers and Henry Holland.

Breakthrough

In October 1788, Soane landed the job which changed the nature of his career. With the prime minister and several directors of the Bank of England already clients of his, he was in an excellent position to pick up the post of architect to the Bank of England on the death of Sir Robert Taylor, who had been enlarging the Bank's premises on Threadneedle Street. For 20 years, Soane oversaw the rebuilding and extension of the Bank in what is generally regarded as his major work. The rapid growth of its buildings resulted not only from an expansion of commercial activity but more specifically from the dramatically increased level of the National Debt brought about by continuing wars with France.

In 1790 came the first of a series of appointments connected with the Palace of Westminster. These led to a frustrating series of opportunities, most of which were snatched away at the last minute, primarily by his rival James Wyatt. In these internecine wrangles, Soane did not always help himself, tending to try to secure a result through the back doors of intercession by his influential clients. Eventually, in 1794 a committee of the House of Lords asked Soane to make some proposals for the rebuilding of the House of Lords. From the summer of 1794 into 1795, Soane's office prepared a series of 217 plans and perspectives for a grand new building surrounding the medieval Westminster Hall and St Stephen's Chapel (see Plate 22.9 and ◎CD-ROM 19, CD-ROM 18, Breakfast Parlour, North Drawing Room). The design was in Soane's safest and least controversial Roman classical style, considerably toned down from the excesses of his student plan for a British Senate, and he spent months taking the drawings round his formidable array of contacts in the House of Lords, even showing them to King George III at Windsor during one of the king's lucid periods. In the summer of 1795, Soane was told that the country could not afford a major building project during the war with France, and the project was shelved. Soane never gave up on his dream, however, and made sure that renderings based on it or on subsequent smaller schemes for Whitehall should appear every year in his annual submissions to the Royal Academy from 1796 to 1837, even casually displayed on chairs or tables in the renderings of his own houses (see Plate 22.10). Many renderings were also displayed prominently in his house at Lincoln's Inn Fields (◎Breakfast Parlour, Picture Room and North Drawing Room). One of the purposes of the house decoration was, in effect, to provide talking points with influential visitors in order to keep alive the fantasy of one day completing his great schemes. When the economy did eventually improve, it was to James Wyatt that the task of redesigning the Palace of Westminster fell. Wyatt, one of a dynasty of architects and building craftsmen, acquired his reputation with the spectacular Pantheon assembly rooms in Oxford Street (1772). The favourite architect of King George III, Wyatt took over the top job of Surveyor-General on the death of Sir William Chambers in 1796, a post he held for 17 years. Wyatt was prepared to work in a range of styles, from decorative **Neoclassicism** to various flavours of **Gothic**. In the end, only a few buildings were completed for the House of Lords, in a **neo-Tudor** style, before Wyatt's death in 1813. (Exercise 3 in the Activities Booklet, which you will undertake shortly, offers some guidance on these style differences.)

Professional acceptance

On 2 November 1795, Soane was elected associate of the Royal Academy (◎South Drawing Room, RA document). In February 1802, along with J.M.W. Turner, Soane achieved full RA membership after fiercely lobbying the academicians. A few days later, Eliza Soane bid £570 pounds for a set of Hogarth's paintings of *A Rake's Progress* (1733–4), and soon after a group of the very academicians he had been lobbying to secure his election came to dinner to admire the paintings (◎Picture Room). At this time, Soane was rebuilding and redecorating Pitzhanger Manor in Ealing, which he had bought in 1800, to show off his growing collection of paintings and antiquities. For several years Pitzhanger became a well-known salon for artists, patrons and men and women of the theatre. Soane was repositioning himself as a member of the intellectual and artistic elite in London.

Among the guests at the dinner in February 1802 had been Robert Smirke, the painter, whose son Robert had entered Soane's office on the recommendation of George Dance in 1796. Robert Smirke Jr was a talented and ambitious man who quickly won a silver medal at the Academy and who fretted at the chores imposed on him by Soane. In 1797, at the suggestion of Dance, Smirke left Soane's office, having already upset the other assistants by his haughty attitude. Despite currying favour with Robert Smirke Sr for his election, Soane was to bear a grudge against father and son from that time on. Annoyingly, Robert Smirke Jr returned from four years in Italy and quickly began acquiring influential clients, helped by George Dance. Although Soane beat off the challenge of the young man to become Surveyor to Chelsea Hospital (January 1807), this was a relatively small compensation for the drying up of Soane's domestic commissions and his lack of success in London and Westminster. In the circumstances, Soane compensated by investing money and effort in his new house extension at No. 13 Lincoln's Inn Fields (1808–12) and by preparation for his new role as Professor of Architecture at the Royal Academy (1806).

Soane quickly established a reputation as a difficult and argumentative member of the Academy, a notoriously strife-ridden organization. At one point suspended from the General Assembly (along with four others), he was among those who successfully lobbied for the resignation of the president, Benjamin West, in 1805, leading to the nomination of James Wyatt. The latter's laziness and inattention led to his resignation within a year and the reinstatement of West in 1806. Meanwhile, George Dance had been elected Professor of Architecture in 1798 but had failed to deliver any of the required six annual lectures. After hearing that his pupil and friend Soane was plotting to force his resignation, Dance finally resigned the professorship in November 1805. A long and good-humoured friendship thus came to an unhappy end, although the two were later reconciled. It was particularly galling to Soane that Dance felt able to support the career of Robert Smirke.

On 28 March 1806 Soane was duly elected Professor of Architecture at the Royal Academy. The seriousness with which he took his appointment can be judged by the fact that he had already embarked on a taxing programme of reading and translating architectural texts, which would take up much of his evenings and nights for the next five years. Within weeks, he had set his pupils to drawing up the hundreds of large coloured illustrations with which his lectures would be illustrated (see Plates 22.11–22.13 and ◎CD-ROM 20). On 27 March 1809, Soane gave his first lecture, but the series did not begin in earnest until January of the next year. Meanwhile, when the Royal Opera House, Covent Garden burnt down on 20 September 1808, Robert Smirke obtained his first prestigious London commission (see Plate 22.14). Deciding to build it in a **Greek Revival** style, Smirke completed the building in exactly one year, and it was soon being discussed everywhere, not least because of a rise in entrance fees which led to six weeks of 'old price' riots, during one of which George Soane was arrested. Closer to Soane's home in Lincoln's Inn Fields, George Dance was remodelling the Royal College of Surgeons directly across the square (begun in 1806 but still incomplete in 1810).

The first three Academy lectures dealt primarily with the orders and their origins and meanings. In the fourth lecture, delivered on 29 January 1810, Soane turned to their application and vented his spleen on Smirke and Dance by criticizing their buildings (Plate 22.14):

> There is also another practice, if possible still more fatal to good architecture, in many of the buildings of this metropolis. It is no uncommon thing to see one of the fronts enriched with **columns**, **pilasters**, and other architectural ornaments, whilst the flanks are left plain, as if belonging to other buildings, or erected by different persons at different times.
>
> This practice of sacrificing everything to one front of a building is to be seen, not only in small houses where economy might in some degree apologize for the absurdity, but it is also apparent in large works of great expense, both public and private, even in works where in a great degree the national taste is implicated ... And these two drawings of a more recent work [the Royal Opera House, Covent Garden by Robert Smirke Jr (Plate 22.14)] point out the glaring impropriety of this defect in a manner if possible still more forcible and more subversive of true taste. The public

> attention, from the largeness of the building, being particularly called to the contemplation of this national edifice.
>
> It is extremely painful to me to be obliged to refer to modern works, but if improper models which become more dangerous from being constantly before us are suffered, from false delicacy, or other motives, to pass unnoticed, they become familiar, and the task I have undertaken would be not only neglected but the duty of the Professor, as pointed out by the Laws of the Institution, becomes a dead letter, for the Professor of Architecture is directed to read annually Six Public Lectures, calculated to form the taste of the Students, to instruct them in the Laws and Principles of Composition, to point out to them the beauties or faults of celebrated productions, to fit them for an unprejudiced study of books on the Art, and for a critical examination of Structures.
>
> (Quoted in Watkin, 1996, p.544)

His complaint was that these buildings showed a complete want of 'character' because their sides and back did not conform to the façades. We will return to Soane's idea of 'character' later. Here he means that Smirke's design lacked the kind of integrity and organic coherence which you would expect to find in an intelligent person. He showed two views of Smirke's Royal Opera House, Covent Garden that stripped away the buildings on the side streets which actually prevent them from being seen (see Plate 22.14). Soane's remarks were greeted with vigorous hissing and applause, and many present thought that a loss of decorum had resulted. It is clear that Soane's right to comment on contemporary architecture was justifiable – indeed a requirement of the post. But his machinations in the Academy had offended so many of his colleagues that a campaign was quickly mounted to call him to account. A vote was taken to prohibit professors from criticizing the work of living Academicians, and only Soane opposed it. Soane then refused to continue with his lectures until January 1812, when he finally completed the six he was required to deliver. From 1813 until 1820 he delivered either the first six or a second series of six lectures every January (with the exception of 1814, when Eliza was ill, and 1816, shortly after her death). From 1821 to 1831, Soane excused himself from delivering the lectures on health grounds. From 1832 until his death, the lectures were read by Henry Howard, secretary to the Academy.

Throughout 1810 and 1811, Soane felt ostracized and rejected by the Royal Academy. He even managed to upset his old friend Turner by overtly criticizing the latter's lectures. To make matters worse, his relations with the long-suffering Eliza were at an all-time low, due to his refusal to respond warmly to his elder son's new wife and to some accusations that he was flirting with a young woman called Norah Brickenden during Eliza's long absences looking after the consumptive John Jr and his wife. Indeed, when Soane made a secret will in 1814, he left Norah Brickenden £1,000 (◎Dressing Room, portrait of Norah Brickenden). Their younger son George, meanwhile, having abandoned all interest in completing his degree or persevering in a medical education, had married into a theatrical family and had declared his intention of making a living on the stage. Neither Eliza nor John Soane could accept this, and George found himself struck off with the smallest of allowances. Nevertheless, he applied himself to the art of writing potboiling Gothic novels and melodramas, following the example of Mathew 'Monk' Lewis, whose smash hit *The Monk* (1796) had helped establish the vogue for Gothic Horror. Soane did not disguise his contempt for the manuscripts his son sent him, nor relent in his antipathy to his son and daughter-in-law, so it is rather ironic to find Soane playing with the image of the medieval monk in his own house, especially after the rebuilding of 1823–4 (◎Monk's Parlour and Monk's Yard).

After his wife's sudden death on 22 November 1815, many of Soane's friends rallied round him, including George Dance, and the stage was set for approaching retirement for the 62-year-old architect. But retirement was not in Soane's character. Once he had got over his bereavement, he launched himself once again into architectural politics and was rewarded with an upturn in professional activity in the 1820s. He was even largely reconciled with his elder son John, and paid for him and his growing family to spend two years in Italy. Sadly, John Jr died soon after his return to England in 1823. Despite the unhappiness of these years, Soane produced some of his best architectural work: at Dulwich College Picture Gallery, at Chelsea Hospital and in the refurbishment of his own house.

Westminster and Whitehall

Shortly after James Wyatt died in 1813, Soane managed to get the appointment he craved as one of three 'attached architects' to the Board of Works, with responsibility for Westminster. The new king, George IV (reigned 1820–30), was anxious to develop spectacular ceremonial to bolster the monarchy's dwindling popularity, and Soane persuaded him to contemplate a sequence of buildings constituting a ceremonial route approaching Westminster from the west (1822–7) (◎CD-ROM 21–24). Although nothing came of the triumphal arch, new royal palace and sepulchral church for the Duke of York, Soane was able to design a sequence of spaces for the king to follow, from a new entrance arch and royal staircase (which Soane referred to as the 'Scala Regia' with reference to the staircase in the Vatican – see Plate 22.15 and ◎CD-ROM 25, as built), along a sequence of top-lit galleries to his seat in the House of Lords (◎CD-ROM 26). George IV also approved a commission to build a series of Law Courts around Westminster Hall (1820–6), in which Soane's brilliant planning, cunning lighting arrangements and sensitive attempts to mix classical and Tudor detailing were much admired by architects but frequently criticized by their users (◎CD-ROM 28 and CD-ROM 27).

A group of MPs objected strongly to the neo-Palladian façade Soane began building for the Law Courts and managed to force him to demolish it and rebuild it in a neo-Tudor style (◎CD-ROM 29 and CD-ROM 30). Soane was also enabled to build a lavish Privy Council Chamber, with a spectacular suspended ceiling in 1823 (Plate 22.16), which formed part of a long façade facing Whitehall next to Downing Street (◎CD-ROM 31). Soane envisaged a more elaborate replanning, with two triumphal arches celebrating victory on land and sea over the French at each end of Downing Street, but this was not executed (◎CD-ROM 23). Soane was clearly proud of these contributions to national life and displayed models and drawings throughout his house and museum (◎Dining Room, Picture Room, North Drawing Room), but they have not attracted very positive judgements from most historians since. It is as if Soane's aching ambition to win the very highest honours and put into built form his vision of a new Britain warped his better judgement as an architect.

Soane's work for the Freemasons, on the other hand, was as fresh and innovative as any of his late work. Elected to the Grand Master's Lodge on 25 November 1813, he was initiated on 1 December and became Grand Superintendent of Works on the 27th, when he presented them with an Ark for the Masonic Covenant to celebrate the foundation of the new United Grand Lodge (Plate 22.17). The conventional Biblical Ark records God's instruction to Moses in the Bible to make a receptacle to contain God's Testimony, made of acacia wood and flanked by two cherubim. The Ark Soane designed was a miniature monument in which the three classical orders (**Doric**, **Ionic** and **Corinthian**) stood for strength, wisdom and beauty. As J.E. Taylor writes, 'Seldom has any initiate been propelled so quickly into the upper ranks of Freemasonry as was Sir John Soane' (1982, quoted in Watkin, 1996, p.423). Between 1826 and 1828 he designed a new Hall for the Freemasons, with a sensational ceiling which appears to hover above invisible supports (Plate 22.18). Sometimes referred to as the religion of the Enlightenment, Freemasonry clearly appealed to Soane's need for security and belonging. He had himself painted in his Masonic robes and was a generous contributor to Masonic charities, even paying £500 of the cost of his own rebuilding of the Council Chamber.

Accumulation of honours

We have seen that the exhibition in the Royal Academy of spectacular painted renderings of Soane's designs and buildings was a key feature of his public presence. At first, Soane relied on his assistants to produce these works, but after 1797 he began to commission the brilliant but melancholic Joseph Michael Gandy (1771–1843) on a regular basis. Gandy had won silver and gold medals at the Royal Academy (1789 and 1790), having begun his career in James Wyatt's office. After a trip to Italy in the company of C.H. Tatham (who put together the collection of antiquities which Soane later acquired from Henry Holland's estate), Gandy returned to England in 1797 and tried unsuccessfully to establish an architectural practice. Soane quickly realized Gandy's potential and gave him enough work to support his large family. In addition to the renderings commissioned by Soane, Gandy produced a stream of highly Romantic architectural fantasies inspired by Turner and Piranesi and a literary imagination nourished by Coleridge and Byron. In 1818 Gandy's large painting of Soane's buildings was exhibited in the Royal Academy and was generously received as an accolade for a lifetime's achievement (see Plate 22.19). You can get a closer look at this watercolour on the video (band 4, activity 2) in the next exercise.

EXERCISE Do Exercise 2 in the Activities Booklet now.

In 1820 Gandy exhibited his companion piece, *Architectural Visions of Early Fancy ... in the Evening of Life*, showing a youthful Soane indicating all his unbuilt dreams of monuments and palaces (see Plate 22.20). These were given pride of place in the ◎Picture Room. In November 1821, Soane added membership of the Royal Society to his various distinctions, and his architectural career picked up with another round of new work at the Bank, three churches ordered by Act of Parliament in 1818, two more house designs (Wotton House and Pell Wall) and renewed activity at Whitehall. In 1828 Sir Thomas Lawrence, president of the Royal Academy, painted his portrait as one of his last commissions; in 1829 Tsar Nicholas I gave him a diamond ring after visiting the Bank of England, and in 1831 Soane was knighted. In 1833 Soane's plan to have his house incorporated as a museum was debated in Parliament and eventually passed into law. On 20 June 1835 Soane was presented with a gold medal from the architects of England by 350 subscribers. At a 'Soane Festival' in the Freemasons' Hall that evening, Chantrey's bust of Soane (◎Dome, Chantrey bust) was displayed on a pedestal amid busts of Vitruvius, Palladio, Michelangelo, Inigo Jones, Christopher Wren and Robert Adam. Foreign academies and the subscribers were rewarded with silver and bronze replicas of the medal, respectively. This, finally, was the apotheosis of Soane's career, generously applauded by his architectural colleagues. When he died on 20 January 1837, a new era in British architecture had begun that would see the new Houses of Parliament rebuilt in a neo-Tudor style after the fire of 1834 and Soane's buildings in Whitehall replaced by Charles Barry's (1795–1860) richer and more elaborate neo-Renaissance style.

3 Soane's intellectual interests and the development of his architectural style

---

EXERCISE Do Exercise 3 (a look at architectural styles) in the Activities Booklet now.

An insight into Soane's ideas can be formed not only from his published works and his Royal Academy lectures, but also from his many notebooks full of annotations of the books he bought and read, including many translations from the French which he made himself. This very full documentation reveals a passionate and restless searcher after truth, but not one who found it easy to synthesize or unify his ideas. At different times he advocated contradictory views, from purist Neoclassicism to a sentimental attachment to the picturesque and a taste for the darker side of Romanticism. Furthermore, Soane frequently went against his own strictures in his built work. This fragmentation of the certainties of Enlightenment thought and neoclassical architectural practice is itself a feature of the dramatic changes of the period.

Soane owned and read most of the works that defined the taste and interests of the Enlightenment. For example, he owned the *Encyclopédie* in 33 volumes, as well as many works of philosophy, history and literature by the leading contributors to the Enlightenment. His architectural reading included the key French, Italian and British works in the classical tradition, and in his Royal Academy lectures he attempted to summarize a vast span of theoretical, archaeological and critical writing on architecture. Soane accepted the view of the Encyclopedists – as well as that of Vitruvius (*c.*90–*c.*20 BCE), author of the oldest surviving architectural treatise – that the successful architect must be expert in many fields and have a wide range of knowledge. He collected books on a variety of subjects and was interested in scientific and engineering discoveries. He bought state-of-the-art time-pieces by the best clockmakers (◎South Drawing Room, Library). As one of the original proprietors of the Royal Institution and a frequent visitor, he knew Sir Humphry Davy and counted scientists and intellectuals of many kinds as dinner guests. His lectures at the Royal Institution were well attended, and by all accounts were more successful than his more pedantic disquisitions at the Royal Academy. Soane also believed passionately in the Enlightenment principle of self-improvement, attending lectures frequently at the Royal Academy and at the Surrey Institution, where he became vice-president, and taking seriously his responsibilities to teach others.

In some ways, Soane's taste was quite conservative, preferring writers of the early eighteenth century to his contemporaries. For example, he liked to quote from the Earl of Burlington, Shaftesbury, Pope and Addison (writing in the first half of the century), and he bought a set of *The Spectator* as early as 1774, making an index of some of the articles in 1812. He was well read in the leading French and Italian architectural theorists of the seventeenth and eighteenth centuries, leading David Watkin to subtitle his exhaustive work on Soane *Enlightenment Thought and the Royal Academy Lectures* (Watkin, 1996). Although this emphasis has been challenged, it is certainly true that Soane never tired of stressing the importance of reason in architecture, constantly seeking to explain architectural ornament either by its origins or by some association. Lord Kames's *Elements of Criticism* (1762) developed John Locke's theory of association into the basis for the view that architecture produces aesthetic sensations by association with ideas and feelings about the world. Architectural forms, therefore, had meanings susceptible to rational analysis and could be criticized if applied arbitrarily. Soane's notes reveal him as sympathetic to this approach but reluctant to exclude fantasy and individuality from architectural design.

Soane became obsessed with the search for the origins of every detail of classical architecture, on the principle that the meaning of a motif can be explained by understanding its original function and symbolism. He therefore believed that all new knowledge about antiquity, whether archaeological or documentary, should be mastered and applied to the study of architectural style. He owned many scholarly editions of Vitruvius' treatise, including the *Commentaires sur Vitruve* (1780) by William Newton (1735–90), which included plentiful notes on the latest archaeological and philological discoveries. He owned most of the important architectural treatises from the Renaissance onwards, but he had no interest in the architectural pattern books produced in quantities in the eighteenth century (despite having written one himself early in his career). Soane also bought lavishly illustrated volumes of archaeological findings, including Stuart and Revett's *The Antiquities of Athens* (1762–1816), funded by the Dilettante Society, and *Les Ruines des plus beaux monuments de la Grèce* (1758) by Julien-David Leroy (1724–1803), who had been Professor of Architecture at the French Royal Academy.

Soane read very carefully the French seventeenth- and eighteenth-century writers who made up the corpus of Enlightenment thought on architecture. In particular, Jacques-François Blondel (1705–1774), Professor at the French Royal Academy and author of the most important articles on architecture in the *Encyclopédie*, was a considerable influence on Soane, as he had been on Sir William Chambers, who had actually studied under him in Paris. Soane translated most of the first volume of Blondel's *Cours d'architecture* (Blondel's published lectures) and incorporated many of the ideas into his own lectures. Blondel taught that there are no safe formulas that might be taken from antiquity or learned from a theory of proportion. Architects must use their reason and common sense to decide what is right in each circumstance, following the principle of *convenance* (decorum) – the title of one of his entries in the *Encyclopédie*. For example, although Greek and Roman temples and palaces incorporated beautiful decorative sculpture and made use of the orders, it was usually inappropriate to use these in domestic architecture because the original meanings and associations would thus be misapplied. Although Soane frequently broke this rule, incorporating columns and varied sculptural decoration in his own house as well as many of those he designed for others, he repeated Blondel's strictures in his lectures and held fast to the general idea that buildings should present themselves for what they are and have suitable *character*. When Soane described a building as having 'character', he meant that, like a person, it had qualities of individuality and integrity, did not pretend to be something it was not, made sense and was fit for its purpose.

In his search for many kinds of knowledge, his desire to find out about the origins of every detail of classical architecture and his insistence on the application of reason to architectural design and criticism, Soane was a product of the Enlightenment. In other ways, however, he was also subject to those forces of fragmentation and doubt that characterize Romanticism. Soane incorporated many ideas we associate with Romanticism: that is, with the primacy of irrational emotion, a fascination with the sublime and an intense individuality. In his 8,000-volume library, Soane revealed a passionate interest in those writers, such as Jean-Jacques Rousseau, who spoke the language of emotions. He owned two copies of *La Nouvelle Héloïse* (1761) as well as the *Confessions* (1783) and several other works by Rousseau, including an edition of the complete works. Soane responded not only to Rousseau's emotional empathy with nature and his celebration of genius but also with his paranoia. Like most of his contemporaries, Soane was nourished by the English tradition for the picturesque, which demanded a particular sensibility not accessible to reason alone. For Soane, as for Rousseau, education and convention combined to blunt this sensibility. He went as far as to note:

> Ladies are generally the best, that is the most correct, judges of works of high imagination and intellectual feeling. This arises from the general feeling of nature uncontaminated with those prejudices of education and manner which artists and connoisseurs are not free from.
>
> (Soane Museum AL Case 179, quoted in Watkin, 1996, p.195)

It is notable that Soane's lectures at the Royal Institution were open to women, while the Royal Academy lectures were not.

Soane also owned and read with interest the authors associated with the picturesque. He bought Richard Payne Knight's *An Analytical Enquiry into the Principles of Taste* in 1805, the year of its publication, and made detailed notes on it in 1806 and 1813. Knight welcomed any mixture of effects or styles capable of producing a powerful sensation through contrast, melancholic or terrible associations, and painterly effects, and he resisted the classical principle that there should be a unity of form in any successful work. But Soane noted:

> Let us therefore be cautious not to be surprised and take that for beautiful which is only picturesque. We are apt to ... mistake picturesque effects for beauties. This is a dangerous mistake. Objects to produce that species of beauty necessary to relish the understanding and fancy must possess symmetry and fitness of parts, lightness, regularity and uniformity.
>
> (Soane Museum Archives 1/165, fol. 5, quoted in Watkin, 1996, p.240)

Soane also had difficulty accepting Knight's enthusiasm for Gothic architecture. This is yet another example of a contradiction between his theoretical position and practice, since he created picturesque ruins at Pitzhanger Manor (◎CD-ROM 36–38) and Lincoln's Inn Fields (◎CD-ROM 39, Monk's Yard), and he collected Gothic fragments from his various building sites with almost as much avidity as classical ones (◎Monk's Parlour).

Soane was a close friend of both Turner and Henry Fuseli (1742–1825), both painters close to the centre of Romantic imagination, and attended their lectures at the Royal Academy. From Turner he acquired a particularly keen sensitivity to the effects of light, noting with approval Turner's lectures on different kinds of reflected light, although he rejected a painting of the Roman Forum which he commissioned from Turner. With Fuseli he shared a taste for melodramatic theatrical scenes.

It is characteristic of this period of great change that Soane was unable to synthesize his reading and that his architecture often seems to be in direct contradiction with his teaching. We shall see that Soane had as much difficulty resolving the tensions between respect for the best models of antiquity and the need to innovate in his own architectural work.

The development of the Soanean style

Soane's architectural development can be seen in terms of two parallel tracks. On the one hand, clearly visible in his student days, was a desire to echo the glories of ancient Rome by constructing great projects in a florid, highly decorated antique manner. On the other hand, in some of his work that is most admired today, Soane searched for an ever more abstracted and simple rationalization of the classical language of architecture. In general, therefore, Soane was a classicist, in the general sense that he believed that the architecture of antique Greece and Rome, and that of the Renaissance, provided the best models for study and that the Gothic style was an inferior and more barbarous phase. On the other hand, he resisted the Greek Revival which became the fashion increasingly after 1800, because (for the reasons discussed above) he believed that the literal copying of forms derived from Greek temples was inappropriate in the design of secular or domestic buildings.

To understand Soane's attitudes, we must begin by making some distinctions between different forms of classicism. The long classical tradition, from the Italian Renaissance onwards, was centred around certain assumptions. The first was that the language of architecture should be based on the antique buildings of Rome (and to an extent Greece). This meant the use of the orders with a 'correct' application of the details which went with them. Many different variations on the orders existed, so that architects could choose, for example, the Corinthian order of the Roman Pantheon (◎CD-ROM 03) or of the Temple of Castor and Pollux (see Plate 22.11, ◎CD-ROM 40 and Corridor) or of the Temple of Vesta at Tivoli (see Plates 22.21–22.22 and ◎Corridor), to cite three of Soane's favourites.

As the eighteenth century progressed, the stress on accuracy of measurement of antique remains became paramount. Architecture students crawled over the sites of Greek and Roman antiquity, making minute measurements and producing or commissioning casts or models of prestigious details. The rage for classical archaeology and the opening up of more and more sites for excavation, measurement and publication went with an attempt to master the complex planning relationships of the great Roman baths and other monumental remains. Neoclassicism is the style label usually given to this more academic (but often also highly decorative) branch of classicism which succeeded the neo-Palladian in Britain from the mid-century onwards. French neoclassical architects led the way in designing ever grander, more exaggerated and more fanciful versions of these huge structures. The skill lay partly in fitting in a wide range of different room shapes, types of vault and size of room while maintaining a unity in the whole composition. And for Soane and many of his contemporaries, formed in the Enlightenment principles of searching for reasons and origins, the difficulty also lay in making the final result, in all its details, appropriate to its function. Soane thus resisted the Greek Revival which, stimulated by the new knowledge of Greek – as opposed to Roman – antiquities, adopted a new style of pared-down forms based almost exclusively on the forms of the Greek temple (columns, **entablatures** and **pediments**) in the simplest possible arrangement. This was the style Robert Smirke Jr adopted.

Gandy's composite view of Soane's *Architectural Visions of Early Fancy*, 1820 (see Plate 22.20), perfectly captures Soane's attempts to excel in this difficult field of neoclassical design. Several more projects in similar vein would stream from Soane's pen in the years immediately after this drawing, as he worked on the design for a royal palace on Constitution Hill, the royal processional route and the Law Courts. But Soane's contributions to conventional Neoclassicism have not been judged as successful by most critics as his ingenious and novel approach to organizing space and the invention of his own, stripped-down ornamental repertoire. To most of his contemporaries and still today, Soane's buildings were highly eccentric in their style.

There is an imbalance between the innovation of Soane's work and its importance in his career. Apart from the Bank of England, most of the projects discussed in the last section, although of paramount importance to Soane's career and his self-esteem, failed to capture the interest of architects and critics (both positive and negative) as much as some of his more modest designs, such as Tyringham and his own house. Similarly, the interiors of the Bank of England, only seen by a few invited visitors, were considerably more innovative than the façades. Underlying these differences, especially after 1806, was the pressure Soane placed on himself to live up to the role of Professor of Architecture. Just like Sir Joshua Reynolds, Soane felt obliged to measure himself by the strict theoretical standards of an academic tradition handed down from antiquity via the Renaissance and French seventeenth-century theory. Like Reynolds, his efforts to master this body of theory and promote it in his lectures clashed with his own instinctively fresh and innovative style. In his lectures he was to criticize a number of his own buildings for breaking the rules of classical architecture or, more acutely, for failing to represent adequately the reasons behind the details of classical architecture. We should now try to unravel some of these distinctions.

In Rome, Soane would have spent a great deal of his time measuring and drawing the details of the orders. Architecture students were allowed to hire ladders in the ruins to climb up and take their own measurements of capitals and entablatures. The order shown in Plate 22.11 belongs to the three columns of the Temple of Castor and Pollux, the first you see as you approach the Roman Forum from the Campidoglio. Soane knew this temple as Jupiter Stator and liked it so much he bought casts of the entablature and capital (◎Colonnade). The Roman writer Vitruvius had given precise instructions (including modular measurements) on how to set out some of the classical details, but Renaissance and later treatise writers had noticed enormous variations in the surviving ruins. From the Renaissance period onwards, architects had struggled to measure these details accurately and understand the rules of proportion which governed these dimensions. Soane owned many treatises and albums of such drawings. For example, he acquired the Codex Coner, an album of drawings made in Rome around 1515 (see ◎CD-ROM 41 for a page from this album showing the entablature of the Temple of Castor and Pollux, which could be compared with the more detailed engraving in Charles Normand's *Parallel of the Orders of Architecture*, published in English in the 1820s: ◎CD-ROM 40).

As we have seen, Soane was influenced by architects like Blondel who put the responsibility on the architect to use details intelligently and find out what each detail originally meant. An example of such 'original' meanings was Vitruvius' description of the origins of the Doric order. According to him, sacred temples originated as simple shrines, based on wooden houses. When the primitive Greeks became wealthier and more sophisticated, they based their marble temples on the forms of the primitive wooden hut. Soane later illustrated both the primitive hut and the details of the Doric order in his lectures (Plates 22.12 and 22.13). In the Vitruvian view, every detail of the Doric entablature had an origin (and therefore a meaning) in the wooden structure of a 'primitive hut'. The **architrave** had originally been a stout beam spanning columns. The **frieze** had originally corresponded to the ends of the transverse beams, with the gaps filled in with clay or stone decorative fillers. The **cornice** was originally the edge of the roof, projecting out over the frieze to throw off rain. It was wrong, according to Soane, to apply the details of this order in inappropriate situations. The writer who had most powerfully championed this purist reading of the language of classical architecture was the Abbé Laugier, whose books Soane read avidly.

When it came to the Corinthian order, too, Soane searched for reasons behind all the details. For example, in the order of Castor and Pollux (see Plate 22.11), he noted that the lions' heads in the cornice were originally designed as waterspouts. According to the sources he read, lions had been associated with water since Egyptian times, as it was under the astrological sign of Leo that the Nile flooded. His source even went on to claim that the lion of Venice had a similar explanation, although Soane's natural scepticism prompted him to note that a more reasonable association was that of the lion of St Mark, the city's patron saint. For Soane, then, it was always wrong to put lions' heads into a cornice in interiors or when the entablature was attached to a wall rather than framing a roof, because the function of a waterspout would not be relevant.

One of Soane's favourite buildings was the Temple of Vesta in Tivoli, near Rome, which George Dance had already measured and drawn a few years before. Soane acquired a cork model of this temple made by the foremost cork model maker in Italy, Giovanni Altieri, based (according to tradition) on measurements taken by Giovanni Stern and Dance (Plate 22.21). This model was for a time displayed at the climax of an array of antique casts in the Dome area (see Plates 22.23 and 22.24). Soane was probably struck by the romantic situation of this little circular temple (early first century BCE) on the edge of a gorge and presenting itself in a picturesquely ruined state. He was particularly fond of the order, with its Corinthian capitals sporting a large flower and its slender columns. He displayed a cast of the capital, first in the Dome area and then in the Corridor (◎Corridor), and he used it in the monument to Eliza's dog Fanny (◎Monk's Yard) and in the *Pasticcio*. The *Pasticcio* (from the Italian for pastry or confection) was erected in 1819. It consisted of a series of very different objects, including an Indian capital and a Corinthian capital based on the Temple of Vesta at Tivoli, topped by a cast iron decoration designed by Soane (see Plate 22.25). The frieze, with its garlands and bull skulls, was also a favourite, although here Soane's fondness for the motif caused him to sin against his own principles: he argued in his lectures that allusions to sacred sacrifice (wreaths and skulls) should never be used lightly, for example in domestic interiors. The most elaborate part of the Bank of England façade, the Tivoli corner (Plate 22.22), was based on the Temple of Vesta. The capital on Fanny's tomb (◎Monk's Yard) was a model, at around half size, of the capitals used on the façade of the Bank. The Tivoli corner demonstrates the curious way Soane mixed faithful copying of an antique source (the columns and entablature based on the Temple of Vesta) with his own free invention, using motifs based on antique fragments (vases as well as scrolls and **acroteria** in the arrangement found in **cinerary urns**) linked together with flat strips and abstract sculpture.

Acroteria were used by Greek and Roman architects to embellish pediments, sometimes at the centre and usually at the ends. Often in the form of marble blocks decorated with a **palmette**, they turned up frequently in collections of antique fragments and are to be found all over Soane's house and museum (◎Dome, Study, Monk's Yard, Monument Court). In cinerary urns and caskets, acroteria or scrolls were often combined with pediments to make a particular kind of decorative form in which the pediment stops short of the full span and combines with the sculpted forms to make a unified form (◎Columbarium, Dome, Study). Soane was very partial to this decorative device, which he frequently elaborated into a trademark shape (◎Monk's Yard). Other examples can be found at Dulwich, elsewhere in the Bank and in other buildings.

Soane was not alone in trying to base a monumental architecture on the pure use of free-standing columns and entablatures. A favourite text of his, of which he owned several copies, was the *Essai sur l'architecture* (1753) by the Abbé Laugier. Soane was taken with Laugier's passionate and intemperate advocacy of columns, and nothing but columns, as the essential components of architectural design. Only by using the basic elements of columns and entablatures, Laugier believed, could the true and pure spirit of Greek architecture be preserved. The building which most perfectly approximated to Laugier's views was Ste Geneviève in Paris, to be renamed the Panthéon after the French Revolution. Soane had made a point of inspecting it on his way to Italy, and later used a view of it in his lectures (Plate 22.6).

Tyringham

From 1781, Soane built up his expertise in modifying and planning country houses. Many of his interventions involved subsidiary buildings, stables, gatehouses or dairies, and for these structures he perfected the use of undecorated brick walls, often picked out in bricks or flints of a different colour, but relying primarily on proportion and shallow relief arches. Often he was required to insert a new suite of rooms into an existing house. Here he specialized in maximizing light and a feeling of space with cleverly aligned windows, shallow vaulted ceilings and minimal but telling decoration.

When Soane was able to design from scratch, he was still very careful to employ materials and forms which would minimize labour-intensive decoration and simplify construction. Three houses, Letton Hall, Saxlingham and Tendring Hall, shared unadorned brick walls with generous bow fronts. In each case, a top-lit staircase unified the house plans while bringing light into the centre of the building.

Tyringham (1793–7, see Plate 22.26 and Figure 22.1), for William Praed, a banker in the circle of the Pitt family, was a chance to aim higher. Soane had the opportunity to place the house where he wanted, on a slope above the river Ouse, and design the gatehouse, drive and bridge to achieve the maximum effect. The gatehouse was the most abstract and dramatic yet of Soane's subsidiary structures (Plate 22.27 and ◎CD-ROM 33). Decoration was reduced to lines incised in the smooth stone, and the main effect was the massing of the central arch contrasted with the subsidiary wings. Soane's simple pen sketch seized the idea in a few lines (◎CD-ROM 44). The bridge was cleverly offset (◎CD-ROM 34) to allow a view of the house through the carriage window, and the winding progress up the slope dramatized the discovery of the house. The arrival in the house was the most dramatic yet of Soane's domestic progressions. The entrance façade was marked out by a giant order of Ionic columns (visible in Gandy's view, Plate 22.26, and in ◎CD-ROM 35), with thin twin pilasters framing the corners of the house. Soane broke one of his rules here, by including balustrades over the entablature to disguise the roof behind. In his lectures he insisted that balustrades were only admissible with flat roofs.

The entrance hall (Plate 22.28) was dark and oppressively hemmed in by Doric columns (in the Greek style, without bases) carrying a full entablature of architrave, frieze and cornice, with Soane's characteristic shallow vaults above. The archaeological correctness of the Doric order was contrasted by the innovation of the painted decoration on the vaults (lacking any classical precedent) and a fireplace in which the faintest echo of pilasters, capitals and entablature is indicated by an incised line. Turning the features of classical decoration into almost abstract patterns of lines became a trademark of Soane's more personal designs (see ◎CD-ROM 15 for one of his drawings for the Bank of England). The entrance hall leads to a brilliantly contrived '**tribune**' which from a narrow rectangular base rises through the house to a **lantern**. The effect was to draw visitors forward into the light and then lead them forward into the living room, right to the stairs or left to the dining room.

The word 'tribune' applies to a top-lit space, typically rising through several stories, which often served as a point of connection in Roman villas or ***thermae*** between larger halls. The word, therefore, had a

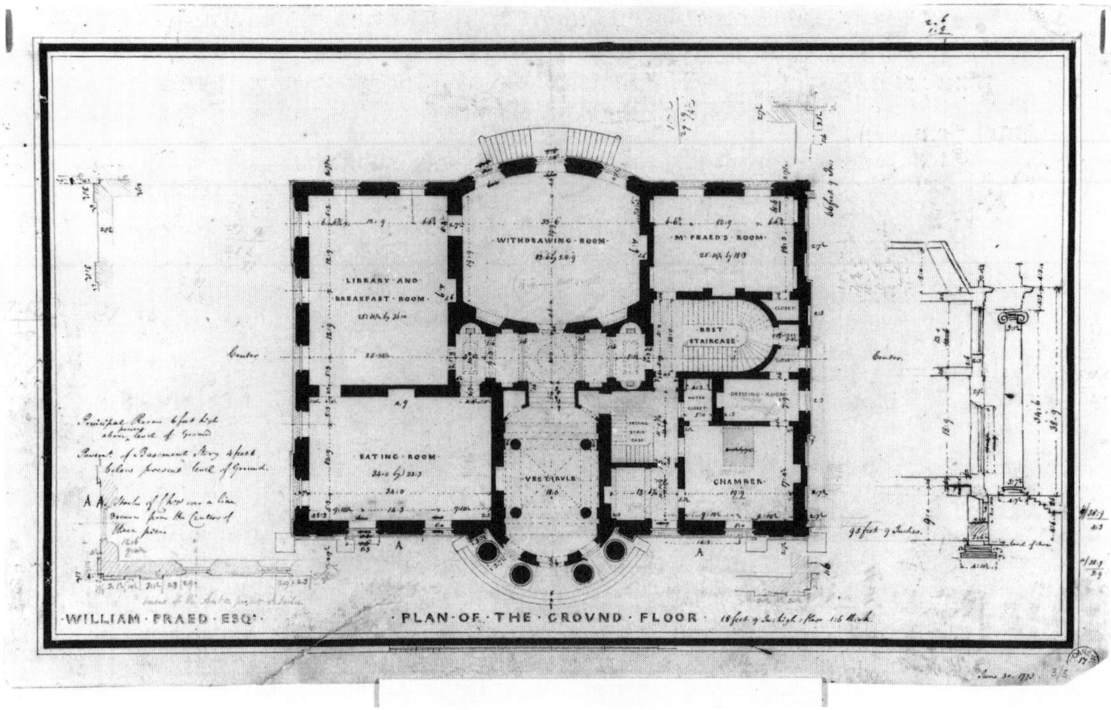

Figure 22.1 Plan of Tyringham, pencil, pen and ink, and wash, 29 x 46.5 cm, Sir John Soane's Museum, London. Photo: by courtesy of the Trustees of Sir John Soane's Museum, London.

potent antique connotation for Soane as well as a practical association. In most of his houses, a central staircase hall performed the practical function of the tribune, for lighting and circulation. At Tyringham and at Lincoln's Inn Fields, the tribune was more dramatic for its compression of space and funnelling of light.

Soane clearly believed that Tyringham was his best domestic work to date, since he invited George Dance to see it. Dance much admired it and once asked to borrow the plans: 'I want to steal from it' (quoted in Darley, 1999, p.109). Tyringham does indeed demonstrate Soane's mastery of dramatic effects, of controlled lighting and the distribution of spaces. Behind an elegant and disciplined exterior, Soane packed all the functions of a businessman's house. The beautiful mahogany model of the house, designed to open up in trays to show the complex workings of the interior, was made by Joseph Parkins (◎CD-ROM 35). It can be seen at the right-hand side of Gandy's painting of Soane's complete works (see Plate 22.19). Soane always advocated the making of models, from elaborate ones like this to simple three-dimensional block models, such as the one of the gatehouse, so that clients could see how the building would look in three dimensions. He also advocated the production of lavish watercolour renderings, often commissioned from the ardent Joseph Gandy, to record the buildings (Plate 22.26 and ◎CD-

ROM 34). Sometimes the views were 'improved' to show the architect's intentions rather than the results of compromises with the client. Furthermore, these views were reproduced in miniature in workbooks, which acted as publicity for his visitors and brochures for future clients.

Bank of England

The Bank of England was the commission which established Soane's reputation as an innovator. By diligence and a careful analysis of his clients' needs, Soane managed to present a series of piecemeal plans to extend the Bank buildings as and when funds became available, while still maintaining a unity of style and a series of working spaces. Gandy's composite view shows a number of the interior banking halls, many of them treated as tribunes (top-lit by circular **cupolas**). In plan, the Bank finished up as a rabbit warren of interlocking spaces and corridors (see Figure 22.2 and ◎CD-ROM 16).

The Bank also demonstrates both sides of Soane's style. The exterior, especially the so-called 'Tivoli corner' (Plate 22.22), demonstrated a knowing classicism closely based on antique sources (albeit with some characteristic Soanean details). The inner façade of the Lothbury Court (Plate 22.29), leading to the Bullion Court, was based on the Arch of Constantine in Rome, and decorated with roundels modelled by Thomas Banks also loosely based on those on the Arch of Constantine (◎Anteroom, Corridor, Dome). The arrangement would be taken up again in his façade of Pitzhanger Manor (see Plate 22.30 and ◎CD-ROM 02). The roundels also appear, along with a set of **caryatids**, in the Old Four Per Cent Office (Plate 22.31). But what astounds in many of these interiors at the Bank, and what has led to Soane's high reputation among modern architects today, is the radical simplification of the space-enclosing surfaces. Instead of a system of arches, piers and entablatures, Soane has unified the whole surface from the base of the **drum** to the thin supports. These supports, far from being 'correctly' detailed like classical columns or pilasters, are reduced to simple ribbed strips (Plate 22.32). To understand the geometry of this interior (and many others created by Soane), you have to imagine a hemisphere, cut into by the semi-circular arches on four sides, and the ring forming the opening of the drum above (see **spherical vault** in glossary). The same principle applies to the vault of the Breakfast Parlour in the Soane Museum, although the arches and vault are considerably flattened and the lantern much smaller in proportion. For a conventional way of detailing a cupola, drum and piers, see Plate 22.6. The entrance vestibule at Tyringham (Plate 22.28) is yet another example of Soane's combination of flattened arches and shallow, flattened vaults. Soane's readiness to dispense with the details of classical architecture (such as columns and entablatures) earned him some criticism at the time. His abstract ornament, incised into the stone or plaster in the form of lines or ribs, was contemptuously described in a satirical poem as 'scor'd like loins of

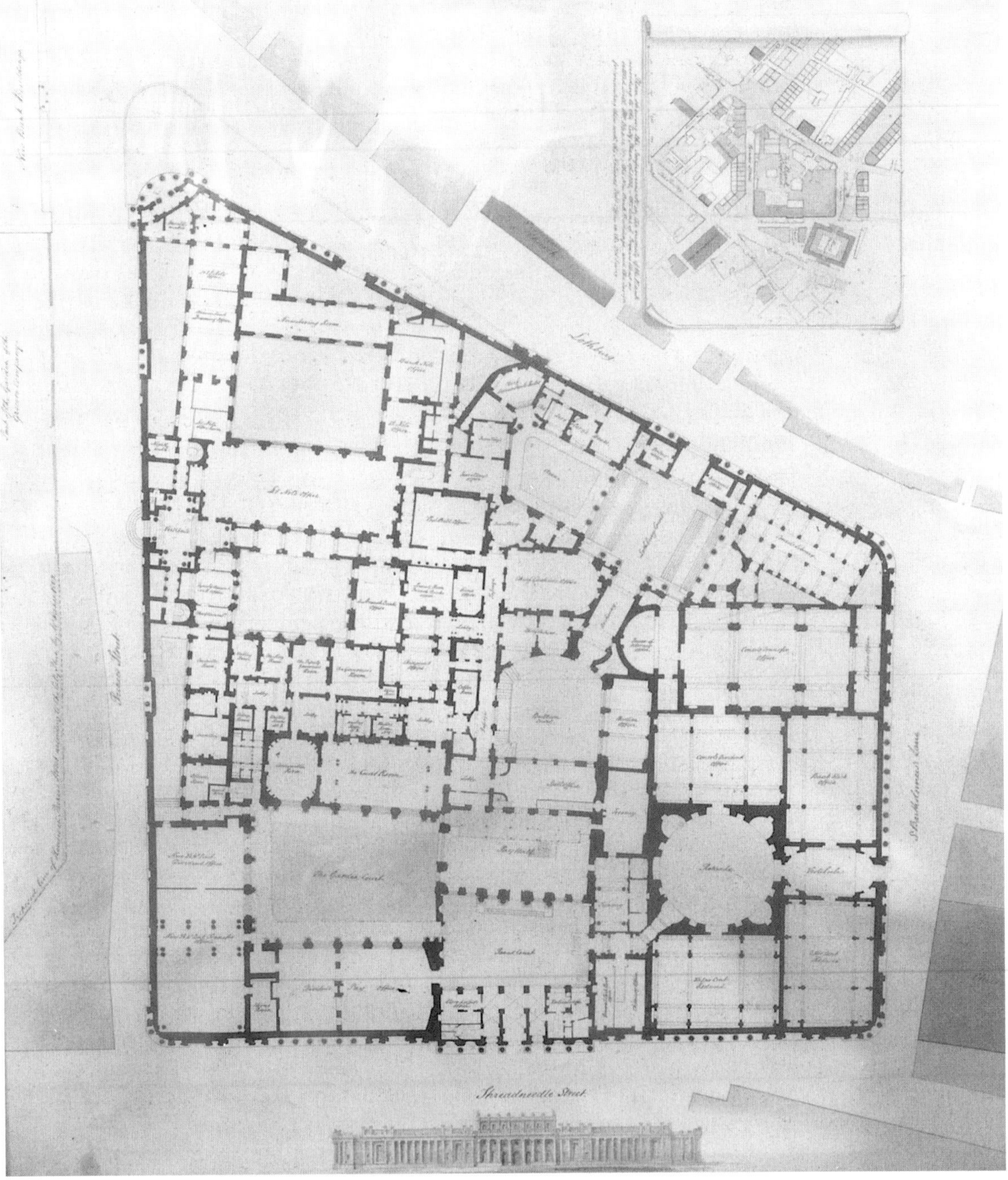

Figure 22.2 Plan of the Bank of England with elevation of south front, 1831, pen and ink and watercolour, 72 x 64 cm, Sir John Soane's Museum, London (Threadneedle Street is at the bottom and Lothbury Street is at the top, with the Tivoli corner top left). Photo: by courtesy of the Trustees of Sir John Soane's Museum, London.

pork'. On the whole, however, his commercial clients appreciated the level of amenity he provided them, with sufficient space and light. And few members of the general public ever saw the interiors of the Bank.

4 The history of the house

I want now to follow through the history of Soane's remodelling of his houses in Lincoln's Inn Fields and Pitzhanger Manor and the development of his collection of casts, antiquities and curiosities.

No. 12 Lincoln's Inn Fields

On 30 June 1792, Soane bought the freehold of No. 12 Lincoln's Inn Fields, a modest seventeenth-century terrace house, and immediately proceeded to demolish and rebuild it. By the autumn, the building work was complete, and he spent 1793 decorating and furnishing the house. The family finally moved in on 18 January 1794. When new, the house must have stood out from its older neighbours, being built of white Norfolk bricks with a rustic brick cornice.

Look at the plan of the house in 1792 (Figure 22.3). Note that the house is oriented north–south, with the Lincoln's Inn Fields façade (bottom) facing south and the back of the house on Whetstone Park facing north. A peculiarity was the party wall with No. 13, which was set back at an angle, causing the staircase to have an irregular shape. The ground-floor plan consisted of a dining room facing Lincoln's Inn Fields (now used as an exhibition space), a breakfast room in the middle of the house (recently restored to its original condition) lit by a small courtyard (Plate 22.33), and a two-storey office at the rear replacing the stables. As Gandy's view of the Breakfast Parlour shows, the decoration created a light and airy effect, enhanced by a profusion of potted bushes and plants placed on shelves in the yard. The office could be accessed from an entrance to Whetstone Park, and there was also a narrow corridor behind the staircase leading to a small anteroom leading into the office. The basement contained a front and back kitchen and rooms for the servants. The first floor had two reception rooms with bedrooms and bathroom above. On the top floor, there were some garret rooms for the servants, which were eventually transformed into a full top storey after 1825, when a third storey was added to No. 13.

From the beginning, Soane's house at Lincoln's Inn Fields had to serve at least three distinct functions: a family home capable of furnishing a backdrop for the reception of distinguished guests, an architect's office where four to five draughtsmen could work all the year and where tradesmen could be received, and a place for the storage and display of books, artefacts and casts. At No. 12, many of the architectural casts were

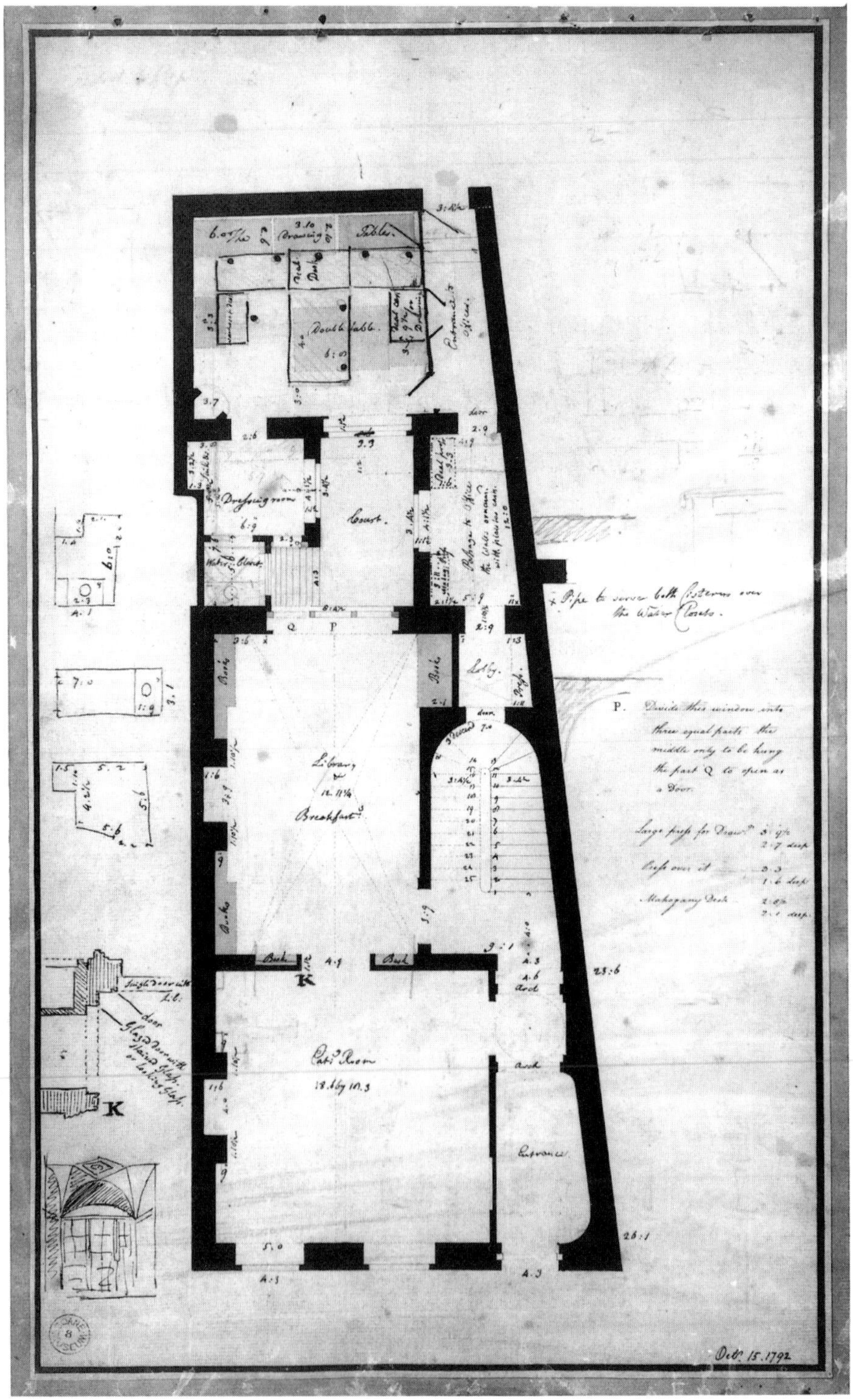

Figure 22.3 Plan of No. 12 Lincoln's Inn Fields, 15 October 1792, pencil, pen and ink, and wash, 48 x 30.2 cm, Sir John Soane's Museum, London. Photo: by courtesy of the Trustees of Sir John Soane's Museum, London. Note: north is at the top.

displayed in the corridor leading to the office from the staircase, and Soane was busy installing these in April 1793. To get some idea of what these might have looked like, go to the ◎Corridor outside the Picture Room on the ground floor. This space is also shown on Video 3, band 4, activity 1. Among the casts displayed here are some of the first ones Soane acquired (in 1792–5), including the imposing cast of the cornice of the Temple of Castor and Pollux and a pilaster capital from the same temple.

EXERCISE Do Exercise 4 in the Activities Booklet now if you have access to the CD-ROM.

In general, however, the interior of No. 12 Lincoln's Inn Fields was kept relatively free of casts and antiquities. This was because, from 1802, Soane began to exhibit his rapidly increasing collection in his country house, Pitzhanger Manor, in Ealing.

Pitzhanger Manor, Ealing (1800–10)

One of the 15-year-old Soane's first jobs as apprentice draughtsman was to work on the extension to Thomas Gurnell's house designed by his master George Dance. In May 1800 Soane had already paid for a plot of land in Acton on which to build a suburban villa. But when he heard of the sale of Gurnell's estate in 1800, he quickly offloaded the Acton site and bought the Pitzhanger estate for £4,500. By 1800, Soane was a wealthy man. His earnings that year amounted to £11,695[7] (Darley, 1999, p.151), of which around £2,000 was unearned income from assets or properties left him by his father-in-law. His salary from the Bank of England alone was worth over £2,000 per year.

Leaving the two-storey Dance wing untouched (on the left in Plate 22.30), Soane rebuilt the core of the old house, fronting it with an unusual portico of Ionic columns whose entablatures projected out from the wall, as in a Roman triumphal arch. Four identical Coade stone[8] statues of women completed the portico and recalled the similar motif on the Lothbury Arch in the Bank of England (Plate 22.29). The Lothbury Arch was specifically based on the Arch of Constantine in Rome, with its circular reliefs and its Corinthian columns breaking forward in a similar way. Soane's idea at Pitzhanger was not only to advertise a design of which he was justly proud (and which the public could not normally see), but also to make claims for his villa, and himself, as noble by

[7] Around £300,000 in the currency of today.

[8] An artificial stone like fine concrete.

association with Roman antiquity. We have seen that he had changed his family name from Soan to Soane and had registered a coat of arms in 1784. Soane also incorporated a number of pseudo-antique decorative elements into the façade: a relief in imitation of a sarcophagus and a number of acroteria. In an elevation drawing of 23 October 1800 (see Plate 22.30), Soane also included a rectangular relief panel in the centre, featuring a luxuriant swag or festoon, similar to the cast from the Roman Pantheon which, as we have seen, Soane already owned and would deploy in the Museum (◎Dome, Pantheon festoon). The drawing also shows two urns on the parapet and two eagles in wreaths based on those on the façade of the church of SS Apostoli in Rome.

The plan shows an ingenious sequence of rooms, from an entrance hall lit by a lantern and forming a tribune with a Breakfast Room at the right (north), a Library in the north-west corner and a Drawing Room on the north-east side. The main axis was taken up by two rooms, the Library and Breakfast Room, in which Soane disposed his growing collection of antiquities. As we have seen, he was inspired by the collections of antique fragments and casts he had seen in Rome, tastefully displayed in niches, sometimes backed with mirror glass. Another source was the antiquarian draughtsman Charles Louis Clérisseau, ten of whose drawings of antique remains he bought in 1805 (◎CD-ROM 43). Like Piranesi, Clérisseau dramatized and romanticized the ruins he drew, creating suitably dramatic contexts in which to place the real fragments he and others had found. For example, his engraving of a 'Sepulchral Chamber', which Soane owned, purports to represent a vast space where cinerary urns were displayed in antique times (Plate 22.34). Soane was particularly impressed by the way the urns and caskets were placed in niches in picturesque combinations. In addition to the decorative potential of this arrangement was the shudder of Romantic horror associated with mouldering ashes of once great figures. (A good idea of the kind of frisson associated with this kind of archaeology can be seen in an illustration from a book Soane owned, entitled *Via Appia illustrata ab urbe Romae ad Capuam,* published in Rome in 1794: ◎CD-ROM 42).

The fashion for placing 'follies' in the grounds of country houses had been well established by 1800, and was indeed past its prime. Most of these follies, however, were of Gothic buildings or castles, which fitted the traditions of the picturesque and accorded well with the idea of association with past events. At Pitzhanger, Soane created an antiquarian folly of Roman ruins, apparently half submerged in the ground, as ancient ruins usually appeared before the accumulated soil of centuries had been removed. This folly would have challenged Soane's guests to reconstruct the 'vanished glories' of an original building. Soane had his draughtsmen work up some possible reconstructions (and these sketches had the specific function of 'amusing' his guests).

In one of his Royal Academy lectures Soane planned to exhibit a drawing of the façade of Pitzhanger, and his notes for the lecture state that the effect of embedding antique fragments was to constitute 'a painting, a sort of portrait' (quoted in Richardson and Stevens, 1999, p.146). As we have seen, the façade of Pitzhanger does indeed boast details of this sort, although the fragments are casts or new work rather than antique fragments. But the phrase 'a sort of portrait' is intriguing. The portrait must be of himself: the play with antique forms and building types included in this façade can only constitute a portrait if we think of architectural reference as intensely personal – a search for truth as much as a search for authority and intellectual distinction. We will see how, as the idea for Soane's Museum developed, the idea of the house and collection as a self-portrait gathered momentum.

Designing the Museum and Dome area behind No. 13 Lincoln's Inn Fields (1808–11)

In the summer of 1807, Soane began to negotiate with his neighbours, George and Margaret Tyndale, to purchase No. 13 Lincoln's Inn Fields. His intention at first was to buy and use the stable area at the back to create a suite of spaces to accommodate his library, his professional practice and, in between, a 'Museum' in which to display his collection of casts and antique fragments. It is no accident that his campaign to become the new Professor of Architecture at the Royal Academy had finally borne fruit (on 28 March 1806). Soane was hard at work preparing his lecture series, the first of which was delivered on 27 March 1809. His draughtsmen were drawing and colouring the large renderings of ancient and modern buildings which would illustrate these lectures. Soane was already thinking about the lack of good specimens of architectural detail available for students to copy, and was accelerating his purchases of casts from antique ruins. Thus, while Pitzhanger was the right place to receive the now large collection of urns – he bought another 40 antique vases in 1802 – and his growing collection of paintings – his wife had successfully bid for Hogarth's *A Rake's Progress* in the same year – it seemed to Soane that the right place for the architectural fragments and casts was going to be central London, close to the Royal Academy.

While waiting for the sale of No. 13 to go through, Soane sketched a first plan for his extension to No. 12 (see Plate 22.35).

EXERCISE Do Exercise 5 in the Activities Booklet now.

The basic arrangement shown in Plate 22.35 informed the projects which followed. The key practical features were a three-storey exhibition space lit by a projecting lantern in the middle, a library on the left side, perhaps with a room of unspecified function above it, linked to a two-storey office building on the right. The plan of 4 July 1808 (see Figure 22.4) shows this arrangement more clearly, with the courtyards at the back of Nos 12 and 13 at the bottom of the page and the entrance from the rear of No. 12 at the bottom left. Figure 22.5 shows this extension as built in 1810.

EXERCISE Do Exercise 6 in the Activities Booklet now.

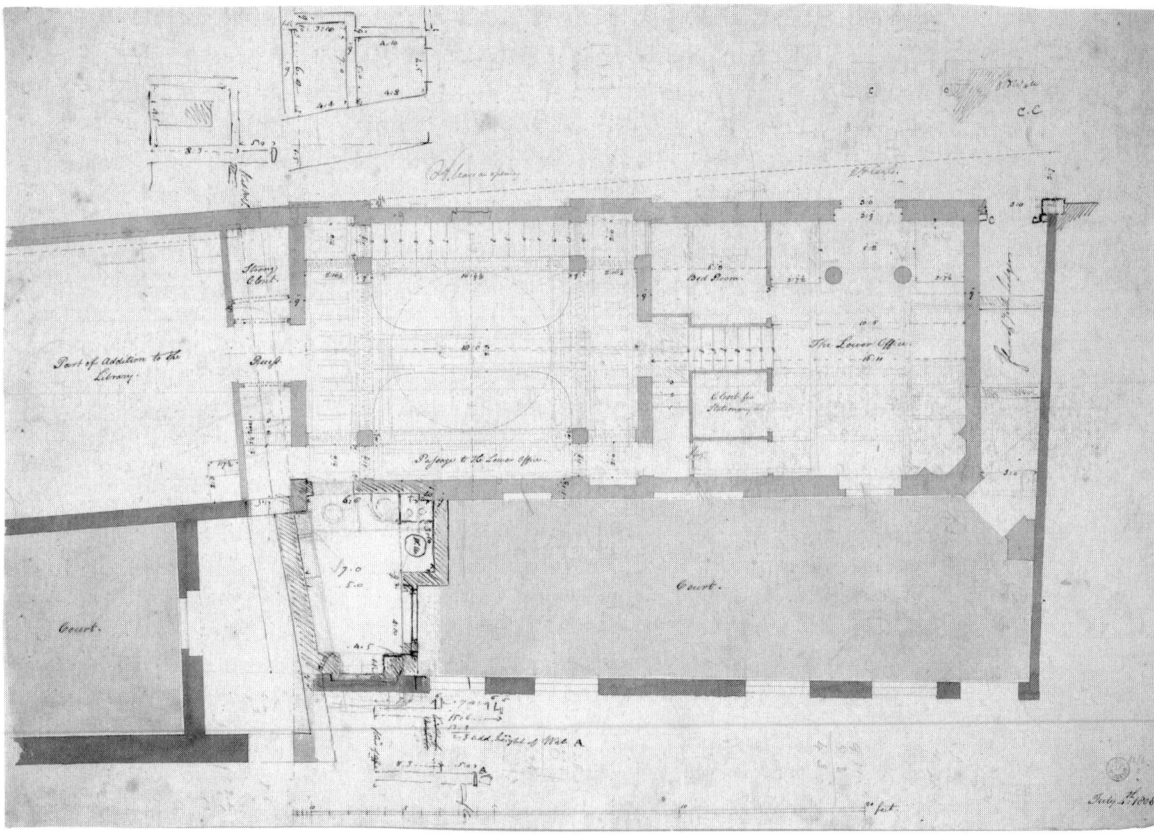

Figure 22.4 Plan of Museum, Nos 12–13 Lincoln's Inn Fields, 4 July 1808, pencil, pen and ink, and wash, 49.5 x 65.8 cm, Sir John Soane's Museum, London. Photo: by courtesy of the Trustees of Sir John Soane's Museum, London. Note: north is at the top.

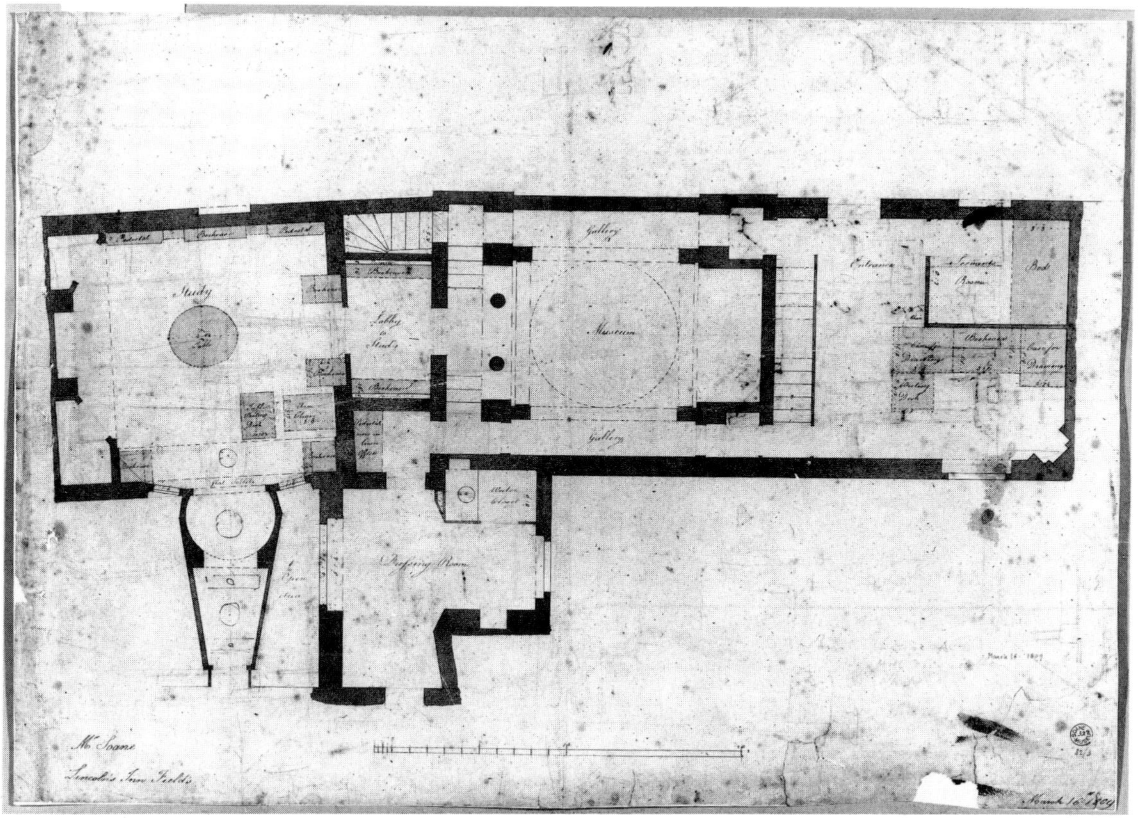

Figure 22.5 Plan of Museum, Nos 12–13 Lincoln's Inn Fields, 16 March 1809, pencil, pen and ink, and wash, 48.4 x 67.7 cm, Sir John Soane's Museum, London. Photo: by courtesy of the Trustees of Sir John Soane's Museum, London. Note: north is at the top.

The rebuilding of No. 13 Lincoln's Inn Fields (1811–13)

In July 1810 Soane sold Pitzhanger Manor, bitter and disillusioned at the failure of his elder son John to take seriously to architecture. The addition to the Museum behind No. 13 may also have persuaded him of the advisability of buying the whole house and making it a more permanent home. Consequently, in 1811, Soane bought No. 13 and proceeded at once to demolish and rebuild it. The plan of the new house (see Figure 22.6) was similar to No. 12 but more spacious and elegant.

EXERCISE Do Exercise 7 in the Activities Booklet if you have access to the CD-ROM.

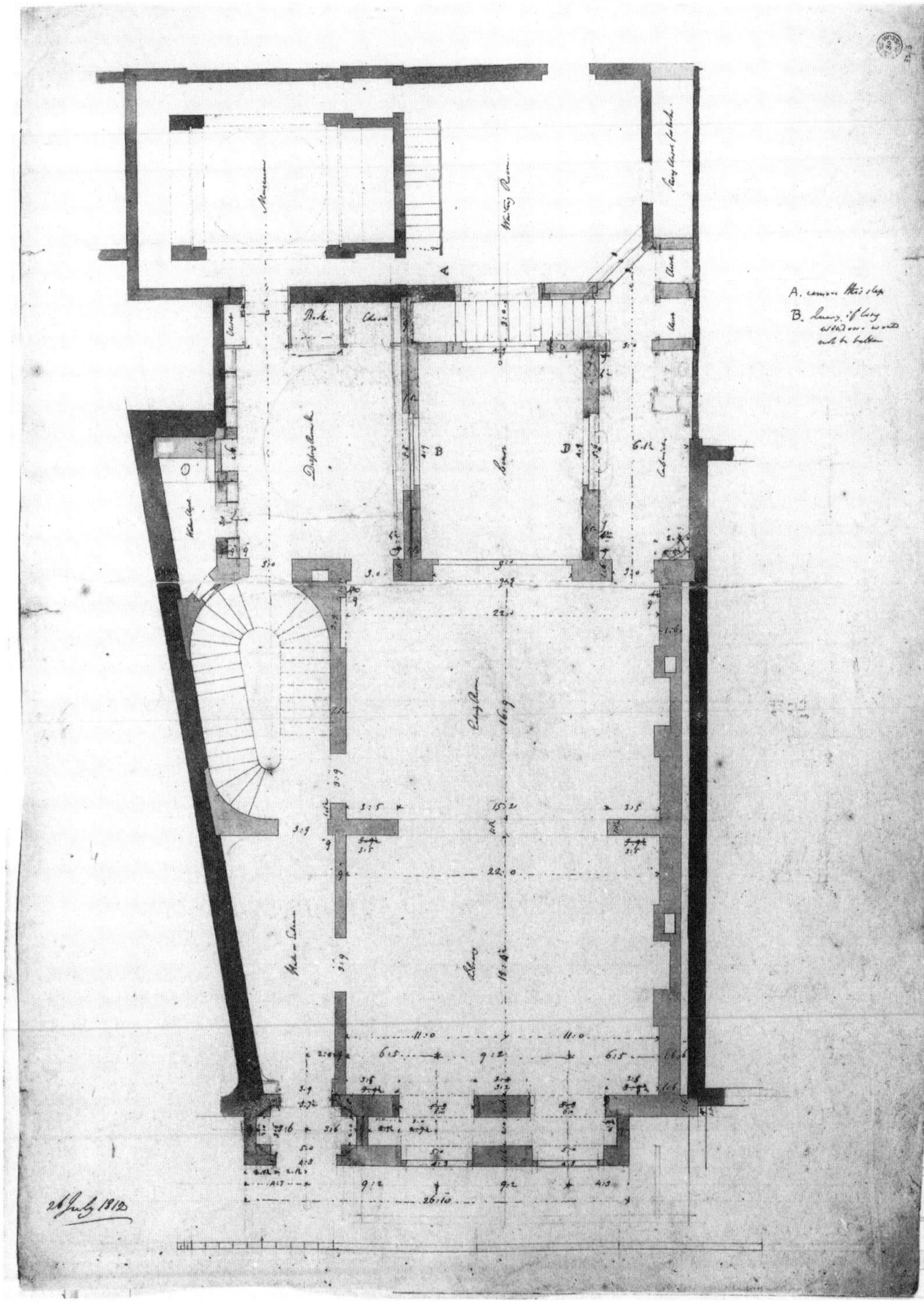

Figure 22.6 Plan of No. 13 Lincoln's Inn Fields, 26 July 1812, pencil, pen and ink, and wash, 68 x 47.4 cm, Sir John Soane's Museum, London. Photo: by courtesy of the Trustees of Sir John Soane's Museum, London. Note: north is at the top.

The Soanes moved into No. 13 in October 1813. Mrs Soane had spent most of the period of building with family friends at Chertsea or on the coast at Margate. Soane himself had alternative accommodation at Chelsea Hospital, where he had been appointed Clerk of the Works in 1807.

The years 1811–12 were difficult ones for Soane. The dispute with the Royal Academy prompted by his fourth lecture was still rumbling on. His relations with his younger son George continued to worsen, and his elder son John remained sickly and unambitious. One consolation, however, was the purchase of a splendid cast of the Apollo Belvedere (◎Dome), one of the most famous of the antique sculptures preserved in the Belvedere Museum at the Vatican in Rome. The original statue was in the news, forming part of a spectacular collection of works which Napoleon had brought from Italy and elsewhere in Europe, to decorate the new museum of the Louvre in Paris. Soane also acquired a smaller cast of the Medici Venus (another of Napoleon's stolen treasures, this time from the Medici collection in Florence). With the temporary peace in 1814, Soane lost no time in visiting Paris (15 August–5 September), where he saw the Napoleonic collection in the Louvre. Another of the works he would have seen then, the Laocoon, is also represented in a small copy in his collection (◎Colonnade). The Apollo Belvedere cast had belonged to Lord Burlington at his villa in Chiswick. So keen was Soane on this piece that he demolished part of the wall to Whetstone Park to get it in. A spectacular watercolour section of the Dome area and newly completed Breakfast Parlour was drawn by Frank Copland in 1818 (see Plate 22.36). The Apollo Belvedere is shown in the middle of the Dome area, with the Medici Venus on the left. (Note that, if this representation is correct, the Apollo was originally placed on the east side of the Dome area and not the west, as now.)

Meanwhile, when the scaffolding came down from the façade (Plate 22.37), it was clear that Soane had encroached on the pavement beyond the building line. The District Surveyor William Kinnard immediately filed a suit against Soane, and was rewarded by some newspaper stories criticizing the stark quality of the almost undecorated façade. Soane would argue that the offending structure was an open 'loggia' rather than enclosed habitable space, and that many of the new buildings on Lincoln's Inn Fields had made similar encroachments. His purchase of two Coade stone statues of women in the style of the Erechtheion[9] (for £40) may have been linked to criticism of the façade, although there were precedents for their use at Pitzhanger Manor. Soane fought the case and eventually won, but at the cost of a great deal of stress, fuel for his natural paranoia.

In the autumn of 1812, with No. 13 Lincoln's Inn Fields still a building site and the District Surveyor demanding that its façade be demolished,

[9] A classical Greek temple on the Acropolis in Athens.

Soane wrote the extraordinary 'guide' to his house, *Crude Hints towards an History of my House* (there are extracts in Anthology II). Perhaps prompted by his membership of the Society of Antiquaries, and certainly informed by the massive reading programme he had undertaken in preparation for his Academy lectures, this text combines a fussy antiquarian vocabulary (using words like **yclept** and describing the Monument Court as a ***cavaedium***) with an intense, brooding and paranoid self-pity. The text includes some passages which take the form of the parlour game Soane had indulged in with his guests at Pitzhanger Manor. The joke here consists in picking on details in the house and interpreting them wrongly. These passages are also a sly means of displaying erudition. Other passages refer to real events affecting the house, such as the District Surveyor's attempt to condemn the façade for encroachment on the pavement, or the criticisms of Soane's Royal Academy lectures.

EXERCISE Read the extracts from *Crude Hints* in Anthology II (pp.189–93). Spend some time familiarizing yourself with the house from the video (band 3 and band 4, activity 1) and CD-ROM. Try to distinguish between false clues inserted ironically into the text to make fun of archaeologists or amuse the reader and descriptions which can be seen to explain parts of the building.

DISCUSSION *False clues*: Soane's reference to the ammonite fossil (with its ram's horn spiral) walled into the parapet of the Monument Court (◎Monument Court) allows him to show off his knowledge of the attributes of Jupiter Ammon, so-called because he was supposed to have been suckled by a goat in his native Crete. The joke about the staircase hall, which is indeed rather dark, depends on knowing that in antique ruins wooden constructions such as staircases normally rotted long before they were excavated. Also, at the time he was writing, the staircase was still in construction. The play on the terrible fate of vestal virgins is a gratuitous attempt to suggest an atmosphere of fashionable horror and the sublime. The reference to the 12 apostles and the niches on the north façade picks up on the characteristic tendency of art historians and archaeologists to find meanings for everything on the slightest evidence. In fact, the relief arches and niches facing Whetstone Park are far too shallow to shelter statues. An intriguing example of a misinterpretation which nevertheless has an element of truth about it is Soane's reference to a burying place. A large number of the antique fragments and copies in Soane's collection, as in many others at the time, were associated with death (cinerary urns, fragments of tombs and sarcophagi, etc.).

'Real' references: As a counter-argument to that of the supposed antiquity of the building, Soane refers to collectors such as Lord Elgin, whose 'marbles' (fragments from the decorative sculpture of the Parthenon in Athens) were to be sold to the British Museum four years after this text;

clearly, this house too was a museum of collected fragments. There are the reference to the District Surveyor William Kinnard, with whom Soane was at this very moment in bitter dispute over the façade of his house, and the oblique reference to George Dance's Royal College of Surgeons on the other side of Lincoln's Inn Fields. More heartfelt still is Soane's reference to the value of his collection as of benefit to architecture students unable to visit Italy and Greece. Later his style becomes more plaintive, in his characterization of himself as so 'enthusiastically attached to his profession' that he is prepared to criticize the work of his contemporaries, such as Dance and Smirke, without thought of self-interest. He then represents himself as assailed by a 'nest of wasps' who have conspired to bring him down. He imagines himself romantically dying of a broken heart under this assault. In fact, of course, Soane was to have 25 more years of active life, during which time he picked up some important commissions. Finally, his reference to his ungrateful sons (the phrase '*filii filiorum*' indicates that Soane was contemplating more than one generation) points to his lost hopes of founding an architectural dynasty.

It was after George Soane had been incarcerated in the King's Bench Prison for debt and fraud (1814–15), his father refusing to pay his debts, that he wrote the two vitriolic articles in *The Champion* which apparently hastened his mother's death in the same year.

EXERCISE Read the extracts from George Soane's articles in Anthology II (pp.194–6). Can you identify aspects of George Soane's criticisms which seem to be reasonable comment on Soane's buildings?

DISCUSSION With much of the first article, John Soane would have been in full agreement with his son, as he had frequent cause to complain of the commercialism and philistinism of many of the people he had to deal with. In his lectures and no doubt in his teaching at home, Soane frequently inveighed against the inappropriate use of Greek and Roman motifs (although he had a penchant for caryatids, two of which he did indeed place in front of his 'brick-built modern house'). Also, he would have agreed with his son's description of John Nash's 'fooleries' (but not of his own Bank of England as a 'lumbering extravagance'). Soane did criticize his Bank buildings, however, in his later lectures, commenting on the inappropriate triumphalism of the gateway to the Bullion Court, which, he admitted, looked as if it were intended to receive conquering heroes rather than wagons of gold. Others, apart from George Soane, have found the terracotta chimneys on the additions to Chelsea Hospital strange, and the term 'raisin jars' has frequently been repeated. Also, the fact that Soane used the same abstracted and spare style for buildings of different functions (infirmary, stables and Clerk of the Work's house) might well have been criticized by Soane himself in his lectures, when expatiating on 'character' and appropriateness of forms.

George Soane knew enough of his father's ideas to make an effective job of getting under his skin. The second article, however, becomes much more directly abusive of his father's work. Nor were his criticisms without some substance. There were many to criticize the extravagance of the new buildings at the Bank. And George has something of a point in his characterization of the Lincoln's Inn Fields house and museum as a 'record of the departed'. Perhaps he had read *Crude Hints*; his use of the word 'ycleped' (old English for 'called', though spelled differently in *Crude Hints*) certainly suggests so. Particularly cruel is his gibe at his father's library, suggesting that Soane, like a 'eunuch in a seraglio', was incapable of reading his books. George had cause to be bitter; his father had earlier made him write a catalogue of his books, which ended when the young George threw pen and inkwell to the floor. Wounding, too, was George's suggestion that Soane was ignorant of the original meanings of the objects in his precious collection, being motivated only by pride of possession and monetary value. George claimed that he, while not an architect, had a higher appreciation than his father of objects like the Ephesian Diana. The final straw was George's selection of Smirke's Covent Garden theatre for specific praise (the building criticized by Soane in his fourth lecture).

Soane was very proud of his copy of the Ephesian Diana, one of his first full-size statues prominently displayed in his new Museum at the back of No. 13 Lincoln's Inn Fields (see Plate 22.38 and ◎Colonnade, marble statue of Ephesian Artemis (Diana)). Soane was so excited by this purchase that he at first displayed it on the north side of the Dome (see Plate 22.39). Eliza was in Cheltenham when these articles were published, but when she was eventually shown them, Soane recorded her in his notebook as saying, 'Those are George's doing. He has given me my death blow. I shall never be able to hold up my head again' (quoted in Darley, 1999, p. 235). On 21 November, she retired to bed with severe pains and died the next day. Eliza's death was a terrible blow to Soane. He gave up his lectures at the Academy and most of his professional work, but committed several weeks to the design of a marble and stone monument in Old St Giles's burial ground (Plate 22.40 and ◎CD-ROM 45). Gandy's rendering of it emphasizes the contrast between the stone surround and the pure white marble block inside. Soane incorporated ancient symbols of rejuvenation, the pine cone and the serpent biting its own tail (this is under the lid which supports the pine cone). On the north face of the tomb, a skeleton hurling a dart (not executed) is traditionally interpreted as a reference to George Soane. Models and drawings for the tomb were prominently displayed in

Lincoln's Inn Fields (◎Flaxman Recess and Dining Room) and in the valedictory painting by Gandy (see Plate 22.19).

Adjustments to No. 13 Lincoln's Inn Fields (1815–23)

Some time before 1817 Soane acquired an important collection of antique marbles from Henry Holland's estate via Holland's nephew Henry Rowles. In the summer of 1816, after visiting the hermit's cell and castle ruins at Knaresborough near Harrogate, he wrote in his diary: 'At home all day arranging papers and settling alterations of the Monk's Cell', and several days later added: 'Arranging marbles' in the monk's cell (quoted in Thornton and Dorey, 1992, p. 26). Soane had written of himself before as a monk, and referred to parts of the basement of Pitzhanger Manor as a monk's cell, but the death of his wife clearly increased the importance of this image for him, reinforced, as we have seen, by visiting Romantic sites such as that at Knaresborough. It seems certain that the 'monk's cell' referred to here was the Study, which was probably reorganized into its two components of study and dressing room at this time. At any rate, the marbles from the Henry Holland collection were displayed in the Study in the autumn of 1817 (◎CD-ROM 46 and 47). It is notable that these fine fragments, best looked at closely, were displayed in this very intimate way. This tiny study became Soane's control centre for the house, from which he could be called into the Dining Room and Library to meet guests or down the corridor to the office to meet tradesmen or professional contacts.

In 1818 Soane acquired a large new collections of casts and antiquities. This prompted him to reorganize the old lower office, which had never been fully satisfactory, as it was rather dark. Removing the staircase along the wall separating the office from the Dome, he proceeded to open up full-height top-lit corridors along the walls (as an extension to those flanking the Dome area). The Upper Drawing Office became an island supported on cast iron piers in the lower office (now the Colonnade). A pen sketch in Soane's hand shows the arrangement of the Upper Drawing Office isolated from the walls, and with its ceiling suspended so as to allow lateral skylights (see Figure 22.7). A view of the Colonnade area before 1823 can be seen in Gandy's composite illustration (Plate 22.41). The density of objects and their closeness to the viewer create a quite different effect from the picturesque displays of the Dome area recorded in the renderings of 1809–12. Every surface, including the soffits (undersides of surfaces), is covered with fragments and casts.

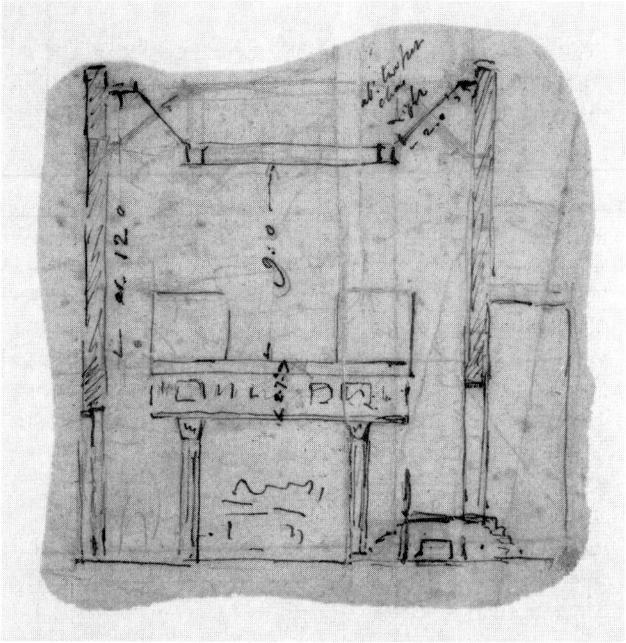

Figure 22.7 Sir John Soane, design section of the Upper Drawing Office, c.1821, pen sketch, Sir John Soane's Museum, London. Photo: by courtesy of the Trustees of Sir John Soane's Museum, London.

The addition of the rooms at the back of No. 14

Soane's eldest son John eventually died on 21 October 1823, after an abortive visit to Rome to collect and draw antiquities. A week before, Soane had just bought No. 14, intending to extend yet further.

Among the new spaces Soane designed was the New Picture Room, dramatically lit by skylights which are masked by a ceiling suspended from hidden supports above. His growing collection of paintings, which now included the two Hogarth series and a number of paintings by fellow academicians, including Turner and Fuseli, needed more wall space than was available. So Soane designed an ingenious system of opening wooden panes, trebling the number of pictures which could be stored and displayed. The coup de grâce in the Picture Room comes when the last panes are opened on the south side to reveal Westmacott's statue of a Nymph, perched precariously on a beam over the open space below.

Meanwhile, after long negotiations, Soane managed to acquire, for the fabulous price of £2,000, the so-called Belzoni sarcophagus. In comparison, No. 14 cost him £1,480. The alabaster sarcophagus of the Egyptian pharoah Seti I had been discovered by the showman and amateur archaeologist Belzoni, who had tried in vain to persuade various museums to buy it. The British Museum trustees turned it down, and

Soane managed to secure first refusal. This coup, which Soane celebrated with a three-day party two years later, gave Soane and his museum great prestige and reinforced Soane's claim for the national status of his collection. The purchase of a second set of Hogarth paintings – *The Election* – in 1823 must be seen in the same light. Soane could now claim that in addition to the antique fragments, the casts and the architectural drawings he had accumulated, his collection of paintings and Egyptian antiquities rivalled that of the British Museum.

The introduction of the Belzoni sarcophagus into the basement area under the Dome changed its character. The funereal aspect became even more marked, and Soane took over the space next to it, which had been his wine cellar, to lay out a gloomy, unlit space lined with niches, into which he placed a selection of his cinerary urns. This space can be seen in the plan and section in the first guidebook to the house, prepared by Soane's antiquarian friend John Britton in 1826 (Figure 22.8). The Egyptian Crypt is to the east (right) of the Dome area (in the centre of the section), and you can see that in the plan it was an enclosed and unlit space. Communication between the Dome and the new extension on the east side was along a corridor next to the Monument Court. This came out to a corridor opening into the Monk's Parlour. This was a fully realized fantasy of the cell of 'Padre Giovanni' (Giovanni is Italian for John). Medieval fragments and casts were assembled to reinforce this association with a medieval monk. Here Soane would invite his friends to tea and tease them with the possible meanings of his collection of increasingly bizarre objects.

EXERCISE Look at the watercolour view of the Monk's Parlour as first laid out (Plate 22.42 and ◎CD-ROM 59–61) and the views of the Monk's Yard outside (Figure 22.9 and ◎CD-ROM 39).

Then read the following description by Soane of the effect produced by the Monk's Yard, and compare it with the description of the Monk's Parlour by his friend Barbara Hofland (Anthology II, pp.198–9). How do they compare in terms of the picturesque tradition and in terms of the reality of Soane's life?

> The ruins of a monastery arrest the attention. The interest created in the mind of the spectator, on visiting the abode of the monk, will not be weakened by wandering among the ruins of his once noble monastery. The rich Canopy and other decorations of this venerable spot are objects which cannot fail to produce the most powerful sensations in the minds of the admirers of the piety of our forefathers, who raised such structures for the worship of the Almighty Disposer of events. The tomb of the monk adds to the gloomy scenery of this hallowed place, wherein attention has been given to every minute circumstance. The Pavement, composed of the tops and bottoms of broken bottles, and

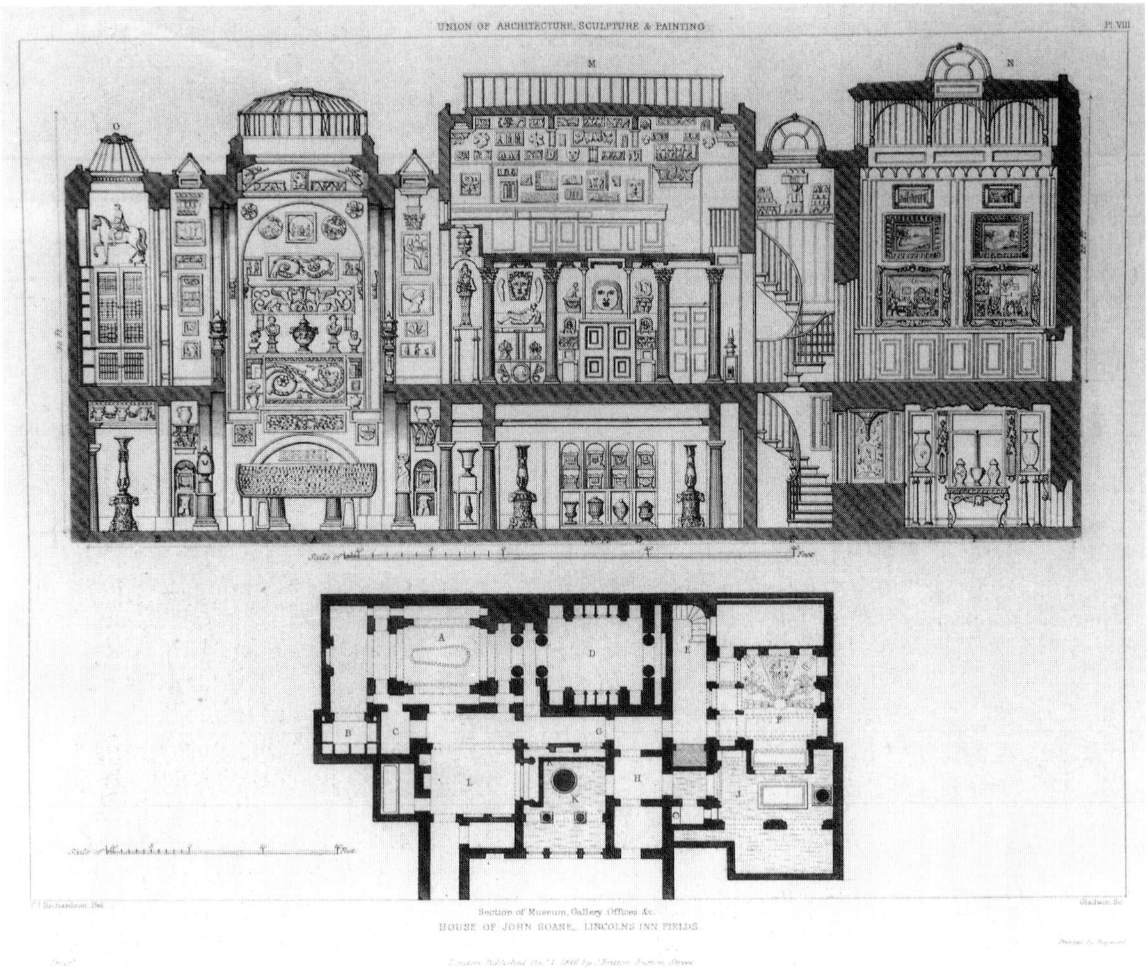

Figure 22.8 Section and plan of Museum, 1826, from John Britton, Union of Architecture, Sculpture and Painting..., *Figure 8, 1827, Sir John Soane's Museum, London. Photo: by courtesy of the Trustees of Sir John Soane's Museum, London.*

pebbles found amongst the gravel dug out for the foundation of the monastery, and disposed in symmetry of design, furnishes an admirable lesson of simplicity and economy, and shows the unremitting assiduity of the pious monk. The stone structure, at the head of the monk's grave, contains the remains of Fanny, the faithful companion, the delight, the solace of his leisure hours.

Alas, poor Fanny!

Amongst these ruins is placed the furnace that heats the water by which the Museum and part of the basement storey is warmed, by means of an ingenious apparatus, the contrivance of Mr. A.M. Perkins.

Figure 22.9 J.M. Gandy, The Monk's Yard looking East, *1825, watercolour, Sir John Soane's Museum, London. Photo: by courtesy of the Trustees of Sir John Soane's Museum, London.*

> It may perhaps be asked, before leaving this part of the Museum, at what period the Monk existed whose masonry is here preserved, and whether he is to be identified with any of those whose deeds have enshrined their names. The answer to these questions is furnished by Horace: *Dulce est desipire in loco* [it is pleasant to be nonsensical in due place].
>
> (Sir John Soane's Museum, 2001, pp.36–7)

DISCUSSION Soane begins with a programmatically picturesque appeal to the 'powerful sensations' to be derived from contemplating ruins. While ruins of antique buildings were usually contemplated as indicating the triumph of Christianity over pagan idols, the ruins of Christian buildings were understood as the victory of faith over time. So Soane draws out the moral of the supposed piety of the monks, when the ruins in the Monk's Yard actually came from the medieval Palace of Westminster. Soane's description has the wry humour we recognize from *Crude Hints*, with tongue-in-cheek references to the 'hallowed place', although in characteristically Enlightenment terms he refers to God as the 'Almighty Disposer of events'. Soane's text undergoes a sudden shift of convention, however, during the sentence which refers to the fictive 'monk's grave' while immediately going on to identify 'poor Fanny' as the (real) dog, his 'faithful companion' who is actually buried there. At the end, Soane gives the game away with his tag from Horace.

Barbara Hofland, on the other hand, while lending herself to the Padre Giovanni joke, transparently characterizes the real John in terms of Soane's own life: his retirement, the loss of his wife and the betrayal of his son (George) who had 'become an alien to his home and his country'. Inexplicably, the other son, the more gentle and sickly John, who had already died, seems to be transformed into a beautiful daughter 'whose tenderness consoled him'. Mrs Hofland does have a sly dig at Soane's assumed character of the pious monk, noting the luxurious furnishings (and perhaps the bottle ends in the yard?).

EXERCISE Read the rest of the passages extracted from Mrs Hofland's description (pp.197–201). Sometimes she seems to be a mouthpiece for Soane's ideas; sometimes she adds a different and more Romantic sensibility. Note one or two examples of each.

DISCUSSION In the first passage, her reference to the Board of Trade and Privy Council offices, and Soane's more ambitious plans for Whitehall, read like a dictation from Soane, never tired of plugging his own unexecuted projects. Her various references to the colour of lighting and its function in mellowing cold marble similarly reflect Soane's known ideas. Much closer to Mrs Hofland's sensibility are the moralizing on the pagan fragments in the Corridor and the vivid description of the three-day party held to celebrate Soane's acquisition of the Belzoni sarcophagus. Her evocation of the ghosts of 'the sons and daughters of a high born race' is particularly effective. We first understand these as Egyptians, Greeks and Romans, and then elide them with the contemporary visitors to the Museum. Her evocation of the sublime horror of experiencing the Sepulchral Chamber alone in the 'witching hour of night' captures part of the attraction of Soane's Museum, not only in the 1830s but also today. It was for this that Soane encouraged Mrs Hofland to write these descriptions, to turn the antiquarian and academic aspects of his collection into an emotional currency adapted to the Romantic imagination.

EXERCISE Do Exercise 8 in the Activities Booklet now.

5 Conclusion

You will have gathered, from Unit 1 and from other texts you have read, that the contrast between Enlightenment and Romantic thinking is not always clear-cut. It is true that there is a clear difference between the mission 'to increase human happiness and progress by the application of reason' (an Enlightenment objective: see Unit 1, p.14) and the Romantic preoccupation with the expression of emotions, sometimes at the expense of reason. But, on the other hand, Enlightenment attitudes to nature, to Shakespeare and to the individual allowed a great deal of room for individualism and poetic sensibility. You have seen that both the picturesque (a poetic response to nature in architecture, landscape and painting) and the sublime (a willingness to respond enthusiastically to wild and terrifying effects of nature and art) were incorporated within Enlightenment culture, although both led to more extreme forms under Romanticism. I would like to end these units by looking back at Soane's life, thought and architecture in terms of three categories:

- the 'hard' application of reason, logic and knowledge to solving problems (an approach typical of the *philosophes* who contributed to the *Encyclopédie*);
- a more poetic response to nature and feeling (characterized by the picturesque and some of Rousseau's earlier writings);
- the Romantic sensibility of extreme individuality and emotionalism (as found in the sublime and Rousseau's later work).

EXERCISE List three examples of each of these states of mind in the work of Sir John Soane. If there are problem cases where you are unsure where to put something discussed in these units, make a note of those too.

DISCUSSION *Reason and the application of knowledge:*

1 Soane's declared motivation in building up his collection of antique casts and fragments and his library was to contribute to human knowledge and, in particular, the knowledge of architects. Almost all of Soane's teaching in the Royal Academy lectures, with the

assiduous preparation he put into them, follow closely the Enlightenment precepts of searching for the causes of architectural forms (typically in their origins), acquiring the latest archaeological and bibliographical knowledge, and seeking always a rational use of materials and planning arrangements. Soane attacked the uninformed and ignorant use of classical motifs, and he also criticized the formalistic and inappropriate use of forms which originally had specific meanings and contexts. In many of his public architectural designs, he used the classical language of architecture precisely and correctly (that is, following antique precedents in the use of the orders and the layout of plans).

2 Soane's library, his reading notes and translations showed him to be an avid *philosophe*, owning the *Encyclopédie* and many other works of Enlightenment thought, literature and architecture. He read and painstakingly translated many of the seventeenth- and eighteenth-century French texts (Blondel and the Abbé Laugier) on which the rational theory of Neoclassicism was based. He also bought the latest folios recording the archaeological expeditions funded by the Dilettante Society and others.

3 Soane was also curious about the latest scientific and engineering discoveries, purchasing state-of-the-art equipment (clock, barometer), attending lectures at the Royal Academy and Surrey Institution, and supporting public education. Soane's enthusiastic membership of the Freemasons and his apparent agnosticism could also be aligned with Enlightenment scepticism and rationalism.

Picturesque:

1 Soane owned the key texts on the picturesque, such as Richard Payne Knight's *An Analytical Enquiry into the Principles of Taste*, and shared Knight's fascination with ruins. At Pitzhanger Manor (◎CD-ROM 36–38) and in Lincoln's Inn Fields (Figure 22.9 and ◎CD-ROM 39), Soane created ruins to give his visitors that shiver of *memento mori* which was so characteristic of the picturesque response. Soane's response to the picturesque comes out in his commitment to painterly representations of his buildings in the highly artistic renderings of Gandy and others of his draughtsmen. The views you studied of Soane's house and museum are not simple transcriptions of architecture, but highly charged and poetic artistic statements.

2 Soane's admiration of Piranesi and of the landscape paintings of Turner also demonstrate his sensibility to the picturesque.

3 In his own architecture Soane's use of coloured light, often from concealed sources, his dramatic use of space and the apparently unsupported shallow domes and vaults he loved to use, along with his insistence on the need of the architect to achieve 'character' in his

work, mark him out as much more than a conventional neoclassical architect.

Romanticism and the sublime:

1 Soane's obsession with death, expressed not only in his designs for mausolea (including his own) but also in the decor and fictive world he designed for himself in the Monk's Parlour and Monk's Yard, is close to the Romantic sensibility.

2 Although we discussed Barbara Hofland's and Soane's descriptions of these in terms of the picturesque, Soane's attachment to ruins (including the representation of his own buildings, such as the Bank of England, as a ruin) occasionally goes beyond the picturesque shiver to the full horror of the sublime. An ardent fan of Shakespeare and a lover of the theatre, he liked the Romantic sensibility of his friend and fellow Royal Academy Professor Henry Fuseli, some of whose melodramatic canvases he acquired.

3 Romantic, too, is the unconventionality of some of Soane's architectural work, including many of the Bank interiors and the façade of his house in Lincoln's Inn Fields, where the details of classical architecture are replaced by abstract lines and stark surfaces.

If you had difficulty with any of this, I imagine it may have been around the grey area which connects the picturesque and the sublime. For example, I placed Soane's follies or ruins at Pitzhanger and Lincoln's Inn Fields in the picturesque category, but later accepted that, in the context of the Monk's Parlour, the myth of the defunct 'Padre Giovanni', and the kind of description by Mrs Hofland published in the later *Descriptions*, these ruins could be seen either as picturesque or as sublime and Romantic, creating horror as well as a gentle poetic shiver in the minds of the visitor. Similarly, whether you consider the Belzoni sarcophagus as a high example of the Enlightenment search for knowledge or as a Romantic shocker depends on whether you place it in the context of archaeology or of the 'Sepulchral Chamber' and, in particular, the spectacular presentation of its opening in 1825, complete with ghoulish lighting. The evocative renderings of the Museum by Gandy and others play up these Romantic associations.

EXERCISE As a follow-up exercise, those of you with access to the CD-ROM might like to perform the same task of classification in terms of the house in Lincoln's Inn Fields. Do Exercise 9 in the Activities Booklet.

Moving on beyond the contrast between Enlightenment and Romanticism, what other features of Soane's life and work can be associated with the 'cultural shifts' listed in Unit 1?

EXERCISE Look again at the 15 headings listed on pp.60–1 of Unit 1 and note any of Soane's experiences, work or ideas which seem relevant.

DISCUSSION

1. Generally speaking, Soane was conservative in his political views, despite being a great admirer of Napoleon. In institutional terms, however, he was a reformer and modernizer, constantly getting into trouble at the Royal Academy and impatient with the amateurism of his architectural colleagues.
2. We have discussed Soane's commitment to the search for causes through the acquisition of knowledge. Increasingly, however, we find a tendency to break his own rules and to rely on emotional sensitivity (for example, in the decoration of his own house).
3. Soane was always highly paranoid, introspective, morbid and prone to depression. To this extent he was a paradigmatic figure of the Romantic period.
4. Soane usually stopped short of the excesses of the sublime in his buildings, although there is always a trace of it in his best work. The sublime becomes ever more present in his interiors, however. You can see this in the way he treats space in his house, alternatively squeezing you into tiny spaces and corridors and suddenly opening views, above or below, in unexpected ways. His 'unsupported' vaults, as in the Picture Room, or in the Freemasons Hall, could also be seen as sublime.
5. This point is virtually written to describe Soane's approach to architectural education and design, with its obsessive search for the 'original' and 'authentic' origins of classical forms. From an exploration of the house and its contents on the CD-Rom or the video, you will have noted that Soane was eclectic in his collecting, including natural objects, Gothic, Renaissance and Baroque items as well as fragments and casts from antiquity.
6. Soane's uneasy attitude to public commissions, particularly those seeking royal patronage for which he had to suffer many frustrations, makes clear his ambiguous attitudes. On the one hand, he longed to create great schemes for the state (such as the House of Lords projects), but, on the other, he stifled much of his ingenuity in order to make his schemes more acceptable. With the secure patronage of the Bank of England, however, Soane allowed his very personal style full expression.

7 In the work of artists and architects, it is difficult to identify cold reason lacking any emotion. Soane's work was always passionate, even in his most correctly neoclassical student projects.

8 Soane was a busy professional and devoted husband, albeit with one apparent deviation with respect to the young Norah Brickenden. His tormented relationship with his sons, however, and especially the highly Romantic career and mentality of his son George, drew Soane into a saga worthy of the melodramas penned by George Soane himself.

9 It is clear that Soane, who travelled widely and continuously across Britain, had a keen sensitivity to nature. Like his friend Turner, he loved to fish and frequently visited his brother's house in Chertsea to take pleasure in the countryside. This sensitivity can be found at one stage removed in the watercolours he commissioned from Gandy (e.g. of Tyringham).

10 Soane as an architect could never allow his imagination to escape completely from the rules of classicism and his knowledge of the architecture of the past. As a writer, for example in the *Crude Hints* you have studied, he was capable of extraordinary flights of fancy. There is also, in his writings and demonstrated in some of his built work, a view of the importance of individual creativity that takes precedence over correctness.

11 Soane's preoccupation with death and melancholy grew throughout his life, but he began designing mausolea for his aristocratic clients while still a student in Rome.

12 Despite courting George III (without success) and the Prince Regent (with a little more success), Soane's admiration for Napoleon clearly reveals him as potentially critical of monarchy. As a self-made man, Soane was critical and suspicious of institutions and politicians, but he stopped well short of advocating revolution or radical social change.

13 Many of Soane's friends and clients were self-made men building fortunes in new industries. Soane himself followed new developments in structure and decoration closely (for example, making enthusiastic use of Coade stone mass-produced statuary).

14 From the so-called Baron d'Hancarville, Soane picked up the idea that all cultures are linked by underlying sexual and religious norms, and thus looked to Egyptian and Indian, as well as antique Greek and Roman, civilizations for sources. He followed the new discoveries in Egypt with great attention, spending more on the Belzoni sarcophagus than he spent on the third of his houses on Lincoln's Inn Fields. He also owned Chinese porcelain, Peruvian ceramics and Indian fragments, including an Indian capital which he

placed in the eclectic *Pasticcio* which formed the centrepiece of the Monument Court in his house.

15 Like many self-made men of the time, Soane felt particularly threatened by the popular disturbances he saw around him in London. He retained the Enlightenment view that the path to peaceful progress was through education and hard work.

Sir John Soane was a man typical of his time in a number of ways. He rose to the top of his profession through hard work and education, and responded to the full weight of Enlightenment thinking, but his restless imagination and paranoia led him to innovate both in his architecture and in the creation of his house and museum. In these ways he was similar to Napoleon but also to Sir Humphry Davy. The preservation of Soane's Museum, and the incredibly rich documentation of every aspect of his professional and private life, give us a unique insight into the intimate context of such a man and the changes in his attitudes and work during our period.

References

Britton, J. (1827) *The Union of Architecture, Sculpture and Painting ...*, London.

Darley, G. (1999) *John Soane: An Accidental Romantic*, New Haven and London, Yale University Press.

Dean, P. (1999) *Sir John Soane and the Country Estate*, London, Ashgate.

Dorey, H. (ed.) (1999) *Visions of Ruin: Architectural Fantasies and Designs for Garden Follies*, exhibition catalogue, London, Sir John Soane's Museum.

Feinberg, S. (1980) *Sir John Soane's 'Museum': An Analysis of the Architect's House-Museum in Lincoln's Inn Fields, London*, Ann Arbor, University of Michigan Press.

Palmer, S. (1999) *The Soanes at Home*, London, Sir John Soane's Museum.

Richardson, M. and Stevens, M.A. (eds) (1999) *John Soane Architect: Master of Space and Light*, exhibition catalogue, London, Royal Academy.

Schumann-Bacia, E.-M. (1991) *John Soane and the Bank of England*, London, Longman.

Sir John Soane's Museum (2001) *A New Description of Sir John Soane's Museum*, London, Trustees of Sir John Soane's Museum.

Stroud, D. (1996) *Sir John Soane Architect*, 2nd edn, London, de la mare.

Taylor, J.E. (1982) 'Sir John Soane, architect and Freemason', *Ars Quatuor Coronatorum*, vol.95, pp.194–202.

Thornton, P. and Dorey, H. (1992) *A Miscellany of Objects from Sir John Soane's Museum*, London, Laurence King.

Waterfield, G. (1987) *Soane and After: The Architecture of the Dulwich Picture Gallery*, London, Dulwich Picture Gallery.

Watkin, D. (1996) *Sir John Soane: Enlightenment Thought and the Royal Academy Lectures*, Cambridge, Cambridge University Press.

Further reading

Du Prey, P. de la Ruffinière (1985) *John Soane: The Making of an Architect*, London, Victoria and Albert Museum.

Furján, H. (1997) 'The specular spectacle of the House of the Collector', *Assemblage*, vol.34, pp.56–91.

Conclusion to Block 5

Prepared for the course team by Gerrylynn K. Roberts

Over the last four weeks you have been studying two 'Enlightenment Romantics', examining their backgrounds, their work and the institutions through which they operated. Davy and Soane were similar in many ways. They were autodidacts who, by means of talent supported by early patronage, exploited opportunities available to them within emerging fields of knowledge to create careers which resulted in personal social advancement. Though contemporaries, there is no evidence that they knew each other beyond the level of acquaintance that operating within the same broad social circles in London would have entailed. Soane lectured to a popular audience at the Royal Institution, where the lecture programme was not devoted entirely to scientific subjects, indicating that the boundaries between science and art were not so rigid as we might think of them in the twenty-first century. Soane was a Proprietor (financial supporter) of the Royal Institution in its early days, and was at one point mooted as consultant architect for the project of converting its premises from a London gentleman's home into a cultural institution open to the public. A portrait of Soane was presented during his lifetime to the RI. Davy presided at the Royal Society at the time of Soane's election to the fellowship. In the early nineteenth century, the Royal Society and the Royal Academy were institutional neighbours in Somerset House, this co-location of their premiere institutions suggesting the cultural status of science and art at the time.

You may wish to consider how the term 'Enlightenment Romantics' helps to characterize these two figures in relation to the cultural shifts that are listed both in your Course Guide and in Unit 1, pp.60–1.

1 Politically, Davy's early associations were radical, and as a science recently transformed in France, chemistry was thought to have revolutionary associations. Whether from conviction or expediency in relation to his conservative audience at the Royal Institution, he quickly became markedly more conservative and portrayed chemistry as supporting the religious and social status quo. Soane too was politically conservative. However, both men were concerned to transform their fields.

2 Davy's approach to chemistry was empirical and experimental, and, like Soane, he believed in the search for causes through the acquisition of knowledge – by experiment in Davy's case. Yet, also like Soane's attitude to his own work, as Davy's poetry shows, he demonstrated an emotional sensitivity towards nature and believed in an underlying force or power which was not susceptible to empirical proof.

3 Both men were self-absorbed and introspective. In his early years, Davy experimented with chemically-induced altered states of mind.

4 Davy responded to what he saw as the sublime in nature, while Soane adopted the aesthetic of the sublime in some of his buildings, particularly in his house and museum.

5 Much of Soane's career was characterized by a tension between classical and 'original', personal forms of design.

6 Soane often felt tension between personal expression and the demands of public commissions. Davy exploited his public audiences for chemistry to promote his own career, while also using his audiences to ratify what was essentially the private work of his laboratory.

7 While pre-eminently an empiricist who avoided scientific theorizing, Davy's response to nature was at the same time emotional and passionate. As Tim Benton says, Soane's work 'was always passionate, even in his most correctly neoclassical student projects' (p.129).

8 Both Soane and Davy had complicated private lives, which were not uniformly compatible with absolutist approaches to morality: Soane in relation to his son and Davy in relation to his wife. They both had engaging but difficult personalities, and neither achieved ultimate peronal fulfilment.

9 Nature and the countryside, including country pursuits such as fishing, were central to the lives of both Soane and Davy. Davy looked forward to a dynamic chemistry of forces and powers rather than inert matter.

10 Both men drew on existing work, but also saw individual creativity and self-expression as important. Davy characterized himself as a 'son of genius'.

11 Soane's preoccupation with death grew throughout his career, while Davy's melancholy and contemplation of mortality became ever more evident during the ill health of his later years.

12 From their backgrounds both Soane and Davy were likely to have been critical of absolute monarchy. However, Soane's inclinations were never so radical as those of the young Davy. Like Soane, the mature Davy was conservative in his views.

13 Both Davy and Soane were dependent on a mix of capitalist bourgeois and aristocratic audiences and/or clients. Soane drew on new industrial materials and forms in his work, while for Davy the fact that chemistry could be applied to industry was one its principal justifications. Interestingly, the applications he was most directly involved with were for improving traditional rural industries and making them more competitive. This applies even to the safety lamp, which helped a traditional industry, albeit one that was fundamental to modern industrial activity of the time.

14 Soane certainly responded to the exotic. Though not sharing that characteristic, Davy was well informed about and drew on science in other parts of Europe, especially France and Germany. While wishing to gain competitive advantage for British chemistry, he retained a universalist view of science as an international enterprise.

15 As self-made men of the time, both Davy (after his early radicalism) and Soane were suspicious of popular action. Though one of the initial aims of the Royal Institution's proposers had been to promote artisan education, this was never carried through. Both men, however, retained an Enlightenment belief in the possibility of peaceful progress for humankind through the acquisition and application of knowledge coupled with hard work.

In sum, the lives and work of both Davy and Soane demonstrate some of the complexities of the process of transition from Enlightenment to Romanticism during the period 1780–1830.

Glossary

Units 20–21

Associationist psychology: the view that actions, sensations or ideas which occur together or in quick succession are associated in the mind in such a manner that when any one of them is subsequently brought to mind, the others are likely to arise as well.

Air pump: a device developed in the seventeenth century which enabled the study of the mechanical properties of air. By the eighteenth century it had become a standard instrument widely used in lecture demonstrations. The air pump can be used to remove air from a container, such as the glass jar shown in Plate 20.1, to show the effects of loss of air pressure, for example. Alternatively, it can be used to pump air into a container to show the effects of pressure higher than normal.

Royal Society: founded in 1660 with patronage from Charles II, the Royal Society (of London) was (and still is) a national institution for the encouragement of the pursuit of scientific research. Though it rather lost its way in the eighteenth century, election to its membership was, as it still is, considered to be an honour.

Vaccination: in contrast to inoculation with material derived from human smallpox (Video 1, band 1), vaccination, developed by Edward Jenner at the end of the eighteenth century, used material derived from cowpox. The word 'vaccine' comes from the Latin *vaccinus*, 'of a cow'. Live viruses were used in both cases. Inoculation was performed in the hope that immunity would be acquired by the subject's contracting a mild form of the disease, though this was not always the case. Vaccination was much safer as cowpox was a mild disease, which none the less gave immunity against smallpox.

Units 22–23

Acroteria: plinths, usually placed at the ends of **pediments**, to support statues, but sometimes treated as decorative motifs, ornamented with **palmettes**.

Apse (apsical): an apse forms an extension to a building or to a space, normally semi-circular in plan. An apse can be thought of from the inside as a hollow space, or from the outside as a curving projection.

Architrave: see **Entablature**.

Astylar: lacking the use of the **orders** as part of the decoration.

Baroque: the Baroque style developed in Italy and southern Germany in the seventeenth century as a more ornate and dramatic development of **Renaissance** art and architecture. Baroque ornament was often exaggerated to the point of the grotesque (see Plate 22.8). In the case of sculpture, for example, Baroque work incorporates dramatic poses, agitated or swirling drapery, and a sense of movement overall. In England, a short-lived interest in the Baroque at the end of the seventeenth century was quickly replaced by **neo-Palladianism**.

Caduceus: the sign of the Roman god Mercury, represented by a decorated staff, also a symbol of medicine (see video).

Caryatid: a sculpted figure, usually female, sometime supporting an **entablature** (as in the side portico of the Erectheion Temple on the Acropolis, Athens).

Cavaedium: (Latin) one of the terms used to describe the inner courtyard of the Roman house and by Soane to refer to courtyards (note that Soanes spells this, incorrectly, as Cavedium).

Cinerary urn: a stone receptacle, either in the form of a vase or a chest, used for depositing the ashes of the dead.

Coffering: in Roman antique architecture, indentations pressed into concrete vaults produced a cellular pattern of rectangular or octagonal impressions. Antique coffering was usually imitated in plasterwork or even painted form on ceilings to give an antique quality.

Column: in classical parlance, the base (sometimes supported by a pedestal), shaft and capital belonging to one of the **orders** (see Figure G.1).

Corinthian order: one of the **orders**, that in which the shaft of the column is tallest in proportion to the width. The capital is characterized by a highly structured arrangement of acanthus leaves and volutes deployed around a smooth circular form like an upturned vase (see Figure G.1).

Cornice: see **Entablature**.

Cupola: see **Dome**.

Dome: may be considered as a vault on a circular base. Semi-circular domes are perhaps most familiar, but domes may also be pointed, bulbous or segmented. The whole structure of a dome (inside and outside) is often referred to as a cupola (see Figure G.2).

Doric order: one of the **orders**, the most squat in its proportions, with an undecorated capital (see Figure G.1) and, in the Greek form, having no base or pedestal (see Figure G.4).

Drum: see **Dome**.

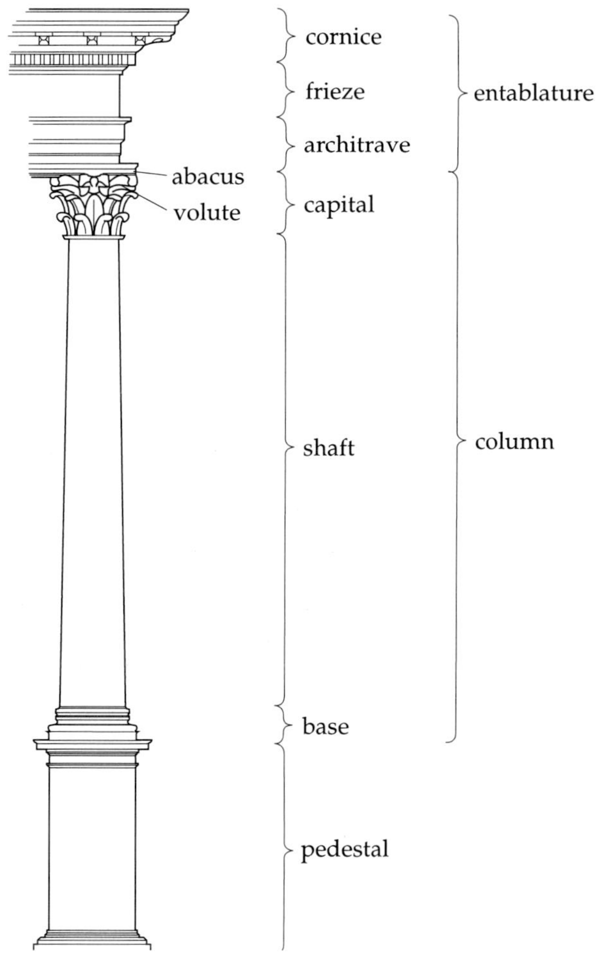

Figure G.1 Parts of the Corinthian order.

Entablature: a real or fictive (that is, simulated) beam, spanning horizontally between **columns** or **pilasters**. In the classical system, an entablature is divided into (from top to bottom) **cornice**, **frieze** and **architrave** (see Figure G.1).

Frieze: see **Entablature**.

Gothic: Gothic was the style used throughout Europe (but especially in northern Europe) which originated in the mid-twelfth century. In northern Europe late Gothic work was still being carried out in the sixteenth century (for example, the Henry VII chapel at Westminster Abbey) and beyond, long after the **Renaissance** had taken hold in Italy. By contrast with the classical styles, Gothic architects abandoned or distorted the use of the orders, used pointed instead of semi-circular arches, and developed a quite different approach to structure, decoration and proportion. The taste for neo-Gothic had already begun by 1800. One of the more famous Gothic complexes in London and Westminster in Soane's day was the palace of Whitehall in Westminster and the

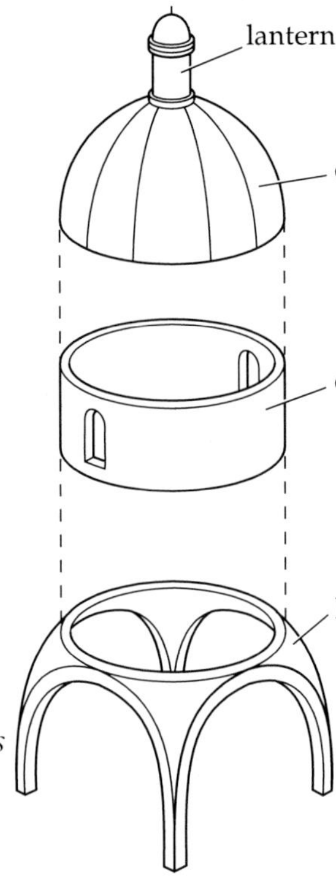

Figure G.2 Dome. Reproduced from John Fleming, Hugh Honour and Nikolaus Pevsner, Penguin Dictionary of Architecture, *illustrations by David Etherton, revised edn 1991 © John Fleming, Hugh Honour, the estate of Nikolaus Pevsner, 1966, 1972, 1980, 1991. Reprinted by permission of Penguin Books Ltd.*

venerable Westminster Hall, which Soane knew well (see Figure G.3). Parts of this venerable building were salvaged by Soane and erected in his house (◎Monk's Yard, Corridor, South Façade).

Figure G.3 Westminster Hall, begun 1097–9, rebuilt 1394–1402. Reproduced from Sir Banister Fletcher's A History of Architecture, *ed. D. Cruikshank, 20th edn, Oxford, Architectural Press, p.479.*

Greek Revival: one branch of **Neoclassicism** which became controversial at the beginning of the nineteenth century was the Greek Revival (sometimes referred to as neo-Greek). Here the aim was to imitate Greek architecture rather than Roman, taking as models the pure Greek temples of the seventh to fifth centuries BCE (e.g. the Parthenon in Athens – see Figure G.5 – or the earlier temples at Paestum – see ◎CD-ROM 06 and 07). Characteristic features were an emphasis, as much as possible, on free-standing columns and a use of a massive, squat Doric order in which the columns have no bases (see Figures G.4 and G.5).

Ionic order: one of the **orders** (see Figure G.4).

Lantern: see **Dome**.

Neoclassicism: a style label applied retrospectively to indicate the effort, towards the end of the eighteenth century, to use the latest knowledge of antique remains and theory to make classical architecture refer precisely to antique precedent. For example, in the 'Tivoli' corner of the Bank of England (Plate 22.22), Soane made specific references to the particular forms of the **Corinthian order** used in the Temple of Vesta, Tivoli (Plate 22.21). The obsession with collecting fragments of antique decoration and showing off knowledge of antique forms led many neoclassical architects to highly decorative forms, especially in the interior. The **Greek Revival** marked a reaction against this profusion of ornament. The decorative aspect of some neoclassical buildings can be contrasted with the austere quality of much neoclassical painting.

Neo-Palladianism: a neo-Palladian style, based on a strict following of *The Four Books of Architecture* by Andrea Palladio (see **Renaissance**), was developed in the early eighteenth century by the Earl of Burlington and his friends and remained influential throughout the century, especially for the architecture of country houses. George Dance's All Hallows Church (Plate 22.4) derives from this tradition, albeit with some personal quirks. To show how a more extreme **neoclassical** architect would detail a church interior, look at Plate 22.6, Ste Geneviève, Paris, where Soufflot has used free-standing columns as much as possible, supporting an **entablature** which runs right round the interior of the church.

Neo-Tudor: a nineteenth-century style in Britain derived from late **Gothic** architecture with some **Renaissance** additions.

Orders: a term used to describe the prescribed ways in which **columns**, bases, pedestals, capitals and **entablatures** were combined in classical architecture (see Figure G.1). The most common orders were **Doric**, **Ionic** and **Corinthian**, although the Composite order (a variant of the Corinthian) was occasionally used (see Figure G.4). The rules governing the use of the orders affected not only the decorative forms, but also their proportions and the width of the interval between columns supporting an entablature.

Figure G.4 The orders in classical architecture. Reproduced from John Fleming, Hugh Honour and Nikolaus Pevsner, Penguin Dictionary of Architecture, *illustrations by David Etherton, revised edn 1991 © John Fleming, Hugh Honour, the estate of Nikolaus Pevsner, 1966, 1972, 1980, 1991, p.372. Reprinted by permission of Penguin Books Ltd.*

Palmette: a decorative motif based on a stylized palm frond, frequently used in antique architecture.

Pediment: the triangular motif representing the gable end of a roof. In classical architecture, a pediment supported by an **order** of **columns** forms the characteristic frontage of a temple (see Figure G.5).

Pendentive: see **Dome**.

Pilaster: a flattened, rectilinear version of a **column**.

Figure G.5 Temple front of the Parthenon, Athens. Reproduced from Joseph Gwilt, An Encyclopaedia of Architecture, *revised by Wyatt Papworth, 1891, Fig.100, p.66.*

Renaissance: during the fifteenth and sixteenth centuries, Italian architects adapted what they could find out about antique architecture (almost exclusively Roman) to modern needs. Various means were found to apply the **orders**, more or less correctly detailed and proportioned, to houses, churches and municipal buildings. One of the more influential Renaissance architects in Britain was the Italian architect Andrea Palladio (see **neo-Palladianism**), many of whose drawings were brought to England by Inigo Jones (1573–1652). Palladio's influential treatise, translated as *The Four Books of Architecture* in 1715–20, became a bible for British architects. Inigo Jones's Banqueting House (1619–22) in Whitehall was designed in sympathy with Palladio's architecture (◎Breakfast Parlour No. 12).

Sail vault: an intersection between a hemisphere and four vertical segmental sections (see Figure G.6).

Spherical vault: referred to sometimes by Soane as a 'canopy'. A kind of vault, circular in plan like a **sail vault**, but flattened as if part of a larger sphere of which only the top part is used. Typically cut into by side arches and, at the top, by a **drum** leading to a lantern or a cupola glazed round the drum (see Figure G.7).

Thermae: (Latin) literally baths; ruins of baths in Rome impressed all visitors by their scale and melancholy grandeur.

Tribune: in conventional architectural parlance, a tribune can refer to (1) an **apse** of a basilica, (2) a raised platform or rostrum, or (3) a gallery in a church. It can also refer to a domed, top-lit area, typically more than one-storey high, often used for displaying works of art. A prestigious example of a tribune is in the Uffizi Palace in Florence, where the Medici family began to exhibit their best antique statues in the sixteenth century.

Yclept: (old usage) called, as in named.

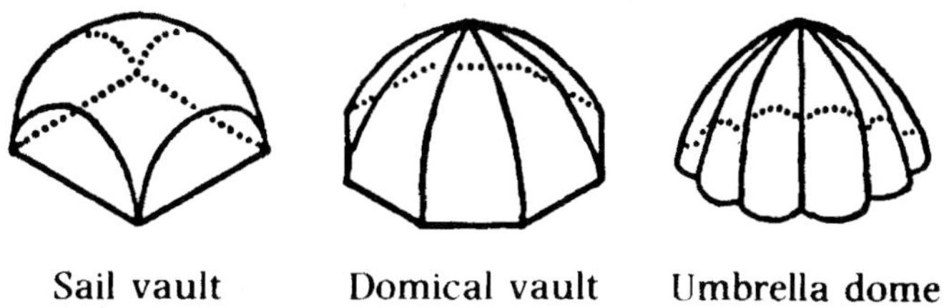

Figure G.6 Three varieties of vaults. Reproduced from John Fleming, Hugh Honour and Nikolaus Pevsner, Penguin Dictionary of Architecture, *illustrations by David Etherton, revised edn 1991 © John Fleming, Hugh Honour, the estate of Nikolaus Pevsner, 1966, 1972, 1980, 1991. Reprinted by permission of Penguin Books Ltd.*

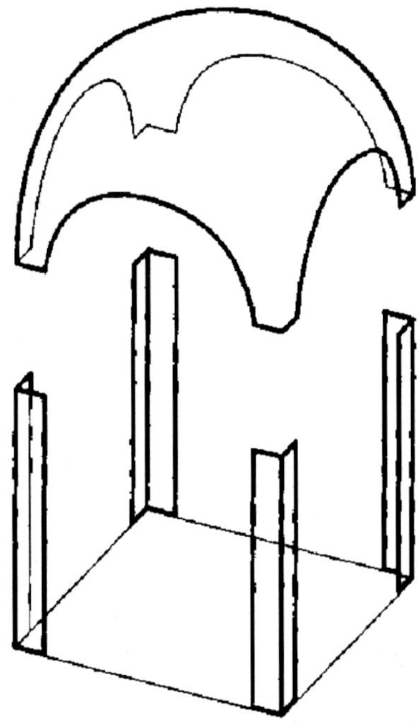

Figure G.7 Diagram of Soane's spherical vault at Wimpole Hall. Reproduced from M. Richardson and M.A. Stevens (eds) John Soane Architect: Master of Space and Light, *Royal Academy, London, 1999. Photo: with permission of the Royal Academy of Arts, London.*

Index

Page numbers in *italics* refer to illustrations.